tabby hunting claws

identity
chipping
Keeping
territory purr
a cat vaccination
Siamese

Viviane Goumot
Yves Goumot

CASSELL&CO

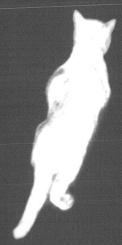

Cats have about

200

million olfactory cells, whereas humans have only **5** million. 79

In the 19th century, British archaeologists discovered more than **300,000** mummified cats in an Egyptian necropolis. 18

In California, USA, one determined cat beat the record for the longest distance covered on all fours – more than **7,000** *km (4,350 miles).* 116

Cat breeds are divided into three main groups according to their shape, characterised on the one hand by the proportions of the body and on the other by the head, face and profile.

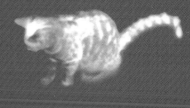

Oriental breeds are of the long-limbed type.
European breeds are of the medium-limbed type.
Persian breeds are of the short-limbed type.

 72

There are approximately

400 million

cats alive in the world today.

 42

'I am not a friend, and I am not a servant. I am the Cat who walks by himself' wrote the author Rudyard Kipling. This may explain the cat's late entry into the human menagerie, several thousand years after horses, dogs and various other

 15

animals were domesticated.

The poor cat has suffered for many years at the hand of human beings. Up until the 18th century, hundreds of thousands of cats were **burned**, **impaled**, **skinned alive**, walled up or thrown off high towers, with the intention of purifying society from **heresy**. To top it all, in England, effigies of the Pope – **filled with live cats** – were burned in solemn processions. Such **cruelty** towards cats has not always been motivated by religion. At **fairs**, it was often possible for members of the public to try their hand at **throwing darts** at a **live cat** hanging in a bag or a basket. ▶ 25

The earliest evidence of cats living with or near people is **8,700 years old** – a cat's tooth found in a Neolithic settlement in Jericho. Bones dating back **6,000 to 7,000 years** have also been discovered in Syria, Cyprus and the Indus Valley. But this does not prove that cats had in any way been domesticated by then.

▶ 15

kittens open their eyes after 10 to 12 days. An adult cat's field of vision is slightly better than that of a human – approximately **180**° *compared to* **160**°.

Cats can judge distances accurately and can perceive the slightest movement.

▶ 79

What should we make of the phobia inspired in some of us by the sight of a black cat? Does this aversion originate from a curse cast 2,600 years ago by a pharaoh against the Ethiopians?

▶ 21

Cats often try to conceal their suffering, but some signs of illness or pain are clear. The cat will hide away, greet you with less affection than usual, and will not seek out caresses. It may also sleep more, go off its food or become irritable.

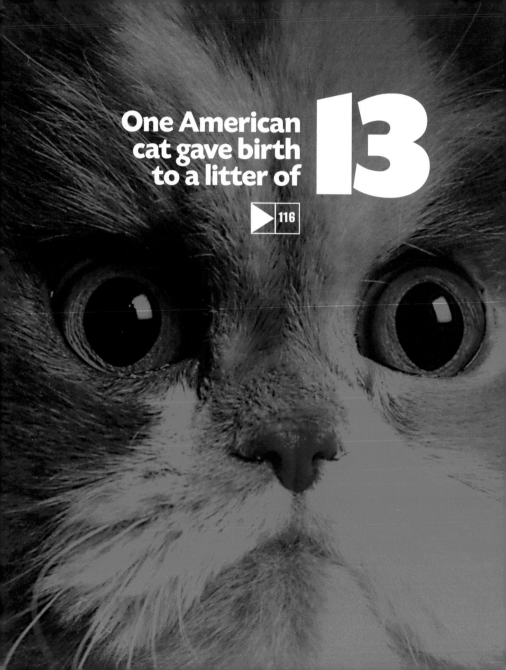

One American cat gave birth to a litter of 13

▶ 116

Cats often play with their prey before, and even after, **killing it**. This may not be as cruel as it seems – it has been observed that this behaviour lasts longer if the cat has worked long and hard to capture its prey. **Playing with its prey may help the cat to relax.**

70

There are only several hundred thousand wild cats on Earth, a number of species of which (like the golden and flat-headed cats of Asia) are in danger of extinction.

42

Cats spend about two-thirds of their lives sleeping or dozing.

If it can go outside, a cat will spend up to four hours each day hunting and playing and, if kept indoors, it will spend the same amount of time doing things like playing with its owner, mooching about or gazing out of the window.

 70

The impulse to hunt is always present in cats ... when a cat sees potential prey moving, its wilder instincts rise to the surface and it will inevitably begin to hunt.

 71

A cat spends about 15 minutes a day eating, broken up into several sessions.

Recent studies of the purring mechanism have revealed that cats do not only purr when they are happy. Purring sounds are produced when the larynx vibrates continuously, which is caused by the cat breathing in and out. Kittens purr to indicate when they are hungry, content or in need of maternal contact. Adult domestic cats continue to use this method of communication with their owners.

 75

Cats love to nibble and, if you give them the chance, they will eat up to 15 small meals in a 24-hour period.

 70

Record breaker:

Himmy, a tabby from Queensland, Australia, died in 1986. He was **97** cm (38 in) long, excluding his tail, and weighed **21** kg (46 lb). He measured **84** cm (33 in) around the middle.

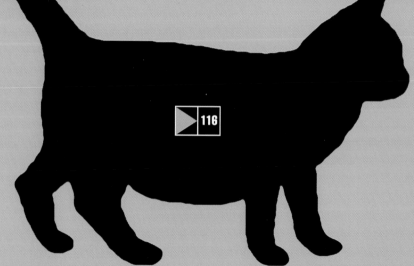

116

DISCOVER

WHERE DO CATS COME FROM? WHO ARE THEIR ANCESTORS?
ARE OUR HOUSE CATS JUST WILD CATS THAT HAVE BEEN TAMED?
THE DOMESTIC CAT CAN BE TRACED BACK TO ANCIENT EGYPT, BUT
ITS ANCESTORS SEEM TO COME FROM MUCH FURTHER BACK IN TIME.
THE CAT'S JOURNEY FROM ITS WILD ORIGINS TO OUR PRESENT-DAY
FELINE COMPANION SPANS 6,000 YEARS OF HUMAN HISTORY.

The origins of the cat have been cloaked in mystery for a long time and, at the start of this third millennium, they are still not completely clear. There is more than one version of the legend that says that cats were created after the other animals had boarded Noah's ark. One version says that cats were born of a mating between a bored monkey and an obliging lioness. Another version, which is equally bizarre, claims that cats owe their existence to a piece of advice given to Noah by God. Noah was worried about the proliferation of rats that were disturbing the other passengers on the ark, so the Lord told him to make the lion sneeze ... and the king of the beasts ejected the first-ever pair of kittens as he did so.

GENESIS
Even though its origins remain cloaked in mystery, popular legend has given the cat a place in Genesis. (Adam gives a name to the animals, Belgian tapestry.)

With few clues, it is impossible to date the start of cat domestication or accurately determine its causes. All we know for certain is that cats were domesticated by about 1500 BC. This much is revealed by writings, paintings, statues and mummies of cats from Ancient Egypt. But what happened before then? We can only speculate.

'I AM NOT A FRIEND, AND I AM NOT A SERVANT. I AM THE CAT WHO WALKS BY HIMSELF'

The earliest evidence of cats living with or near people is 8,700 years old – a cat's tooth found in a Neolithic settlement in Jericho. Some 6,000 to 7,000-year-old bones have also been discovered in Syria, Cyprus and the Indus Valley. But this does not prove that cats had in any way been domesticated by then.

'I am not a friend, and I am not a servant. I am the Cat who walks by himself' wrote author Rudyard Kipling in his *Just So Stories*. The cat's independent personality may explain its late entry into the human menagerie, several thousand years after horses, dogs and various other animals were domesticated. The cat was of no particular use to the prehistoric peoples, who lived by hunting and fruit-picking before they turned to rearing animals and working the land. Cats didn't have a place in our prehistoric ancestors' ecosystems, so there was no incentive to domesticate them. The situation was different with dogs, however, as they could help with hunting, defend their owners, kill vermin and also pull small loads.

It was with the development of agriculture, roughly 6,000 years ago, that the long process of 'taming' cats began. The spreading of deserts, caused by climatic changes, led early Egyptian populations to settle in the valley of the Nile so that they could cultivate the land. The cereals they produced attracted rodents, which, in turn, attracted wild cats. These cats gradually became used to the presence of people in their territory, while the villagers, impressed by the cats' efficiency in controlling rats and snakes, looked kindly upon them.

AS CATS BECAME MORE ACCUSTOMED TO LIVING WITH PEOPLE, THEIR BEHAVIOURAL PATTERNS BEGAN TO CHANGE

In accordance with the laws of evolution, cats have needed to adapt their behaviour in order to allow them to share their territory with humans and continue to occupy their 'ecological niche' as predators.

Over time, cats gradually overcame their fear of farmers and became easier to tame, as genetic mutations made each generation calmer and less volatile than the last. These changes in temperament encouraged the Ancient Egyptians to adopt litters of kittens and rear them separately from their mothers whenever the opportunity arose.

With each new generation, cats became more accustomed to being with people, and lost the aggressiveness that comes hand in hand with the need to hunt. These early domestic

EGYPTIAN WILD CATS

Detail copied from an Ancient Egyptian fresco dating from the 19th century.
(Library of decorative arts, Paris.)

cats reproduced more quickly than their wild cousins, and gradually replaced the latter in urban areas, eventually evolving into a separate species altogether. The physical changes that accompanied their domestication are evident in the 4,000-year-old remains of mummified cats. The gradual change in the shape of the ears, the colour of the coat, the dome-shaped growth in the region of the temples, and the shortening of the nasal regions over the centuries tell us that the process of taming cats took more than 2,000 years. (Scientists noticed similar developments in the peat dogs' skull when they were tamed 20,000 years earlier.)

It is hard for us today to imagine the increasing importance that the Ancient Egyptians gave to their cats. It was comparable to the respect that Hindus show their sacred cows. In a theocratic society, where the pharaoh and the priests held all the power, the lives of Ancient Egyptians were placed under the patronage of a pantheon of gods of hybrid appearance. These gods were portrayed with the body of a man or woman, but with the head of an animal. Horus, the protector-deity of the monarchy, had the head of a falcon. Anubis had the snout of a jackal, and Thoth had the head of a dog. Sekhmet and Bastet, the twin daughters of the Sun God Râ, had the muzzles of lionesses, the faces of a cats, and the bodies of women.

BASTET, THE GODDESS WITH THE FACE OF A CAT, PLAYED AN IMPORTANT ROLE IN THE ANCIENT EGYPTIAN PANTHEON

Bastet, the goddess of love and procreation, was honoured at Bubastis and Saqqara, where crowds of people gathered to beg for the protection of the sacred cats reared by the priests. The festivities dedicated to Bastet each spring were, according to Herodotus, the most popular in Ancient Egypt. But he believed that the orgies, in which pilgrims took part at the time, also played a part in the popularity of the cult dedicated to the cat-faced goddess.

According to Ancient Egyptian belief, Bastet's father, the Sun God, travelled across the 12 regions of Egypt during the day. At dusk, his solar boat would plunge into darkness, escorting the dead into the after-world. Every night, Apophis the serpent tried to prevent the sun rising again by stopping the boat on its journey towards dawn. By decapitating the serpent, Bastet allowed daylight to return – hence the Ancient Egyptians' reverence for cats.

BASTET AND THE SERPENT

The fresco from this tomb at Heliopolis shows the goddess Bastet killing the snake Apophis in the sacred sycamore, thus allowing day to break again. (12th century BC.)

When a cat died, everyone in the family would shave off their eyebrows as a sign of mourning. Killing a cat was punishable by death.

Cats' bodies were embalmed, then wrapped in strips of material before being placed inside a sarcophagus or plaited straw container. They were then placed in a huge necropolis. In the 19th century, British scientists discovered more than 300,000 mummified cats in an Egyptian necropolis. As they did not know what to do with them, the cats were shipped to Britain, where they were eventually pulverized and sold as fertilizer. This may seem strange, but the British were not the first to exploit the cats for financial gain. Thirty centuries earlier, the Egyptian clergy had showed an equally commercial attitude. X-rays of some mummified cats show strangulation marks and signs of blows to the bodies of younger animals. To thank Bastet for her good deeds, devotees would offer her the mummies of sacred cats, bought from the priests as a votive offering. Because they could not always meet the pilgrims' demands for cats that had died of natural causes, Egyptian priests freed themselves from the very strict laws that they imposed on other people. The temptation to fulfil the pilgrims' requirements for cat offerings, and to produce some extra revenue at the same time, obviously proved too much for the priests. They killed some cats to sell to the devotees, who were totally unaware that the animals had met such a violent end.

It was against the law for cats to be exported out of Egypt, so the cynical may ask whether the priests forbade their exportation for religious reasons, or simply to ensure their own pockets remained well-lined.

Over time, the Phoenicians managed to get around this law forbidding the exportation of cats by capturing Egyptian specimens and selling them around the Mediterranean and maybe even as far away as China, thus contributing to the gradual spread of the domestic cat. According to legend and events recalled by the Greek historian Polybius four centuries later, Egypt fell to the Persians in 525 BC because of the cat. In order to conquer the East, the Persian king Cambyses II had to take control of Peluse, a town on the Nile delta. However, the troops of Psammetik III resisted so strongly that Cambyses had to think of another way to crush them. His men attacked with live cats attached to their shields. The Egyptians chose to surrender on the spot rather than risk killing even one cat!

THE ROMAN OCCUPATION OF EGYPT, AND THE START OF CHRISTIANITY, BROUGHT ABOUT THE DECLINE OF THE FELINE CULT

The 'reign' of the cat lasted for almost 2,000 years. Although officially forbidden in 390 AD, the worship of cats left a lasting impression on the history of religions and in the collective imagination of the Western world.

The phobia inspired in some people by the sight of a black cat has proved to be equally long-lasting. This aversion is reputed to originate from a curse cast 2,600 years ago by a pharaoh against the Ethiopians. Popular belief was such that the coat of a black cat implied that it was an intercessor for the dark-skinned Ethiopians, who were considered to be a bad people in collaboration with the forces of evil. This belief persisted, and, in the Middle Ages, the black cat was perceived to be the representative of Beelzebub, the Prince of Demons. Even today, some people still believe that a black cat can bring bad luck. Similarly, the idea that cats carry spells also still remains, a hangover from the time when they were believed to be witches' familiars. A few people even believe that if a cat leaves its owner's sickbed, it foretells the death of the owner. Others think of cats as barometers – if they use their paws to wash behind their ears, it's a sure sign that it will rain.

At the start of the Christian era, the spread of the Egyptian cat in Europe roughly followed the progress of the Roman legions. By the end of the fifth century, cats were established throughout the empire – which then collapsed under the onslaught of the barbarian hordes. An invasion of brown rats followed in the wake of the invaders, helping to spread the plague across Europe. Death was everywhere. Epidemics and food shortages made people realize that cats were the best weapons they had to control the rat population that was spreading this scourge. Domestic cats

THE ROMAN EMPIRE

At the beginning of the Christian era, Egyptian cats were integrated into Europe. When the Palladuis Treaty of Agronomy was published in the fourth century, they were given the name of cattus (or catus), from where the word 'cat' originates.

were sold at the price of gold and were protected by laws like the ones formerly enforced in Ancient Egypt. For example, Welsh laws in the tenth century sentenced anyone who killed a cat to give a lamb or sheep in exchange. If the victim was one of the cats that guarded the royal granaries, the culprit had to hang the cat up by the tail and hand over as much grain as it took to cover the cat's body completely.

At this time, cats were equally respected in the Middle and Far East, in contrast to dogs, which were considered impure. In Muslim countries, cats in general benefited from the love the prophet Mohammed had for his own pet cats. Legend has it that one day, when he saw that his cat Muezza had fallen asleep on the sleeve of a garment he wanted to wear, the prophet chose to have the material cut rather than wake the cat.

In China and Japan, there were laws which forbade people from keeping cats locked up and from trading in them. The presence of cats was considered a sign of well-being that warded off evil spirits.

THE CHURCH DISAPPROVED OF THE PEASANTS' AFFECTION FOR THEIR TALENTED RAT-CATCHING CATS

Superstitious fear of just what the year 1000, at the end of the first millennium, might have in store for mankind, coupled with the upheaval of the Crusades, the decimation caused by the plague and the challenge to Rome by movements preaching religious reformation, all contributed to the destabilisation of medieval society.

The unfortunate cat was to suffer as people searched for a scapegoat and selected this silent, unblinking and watchful creature as a suitable repository for all things evil. The persecution was to last for several centuries. Rumours and so-called popular wisdom were at the root of much of this. Cats were considered to be cunning, clever, hypocritical, gluttonous and lazy, and popular sayings and the literature of the time reflected this attitude.

CURSED ANIMAL

Cats were demonised by the Church in the Middle Ages and accused of all sorts of evils. This made them ideal candidates for being branded the evil accomplices of witches.

The climate of misogyny at the time allowed people to transfer many of the faults attributed to women – who were, among other things, held guilty of the original sin in the person of Eve – on to cats. Cats were accused of colluding with the devil in the kidnapping of children, and participating in orgies and acts of sorcery. Finally, rumours spread by Crusaders returning from Palestine claimed that a cat had saved the enemy's leader Mohammed from certain death by killing a snake that was threatening to bite him. This was enough for cats to be doomed in Europe. From that moment on, they were considered heretics and the massacre began.

CATS SUFFERED GREATLY AND WERE PERSECUTED FOR CENTURIES

In these sad times, no act against a cat was considered too barbaric. Across Europe, cats were burned, impaled, skinned alive, walled up or thrown off high towers. To top it all, in England, effigies of the Pope – stuffed with live cats – were burned in solemn processions. Such cruelty towards cats has not always been motivated by religion. At fairs, it was often possible for members of the public to try their hand at throwing darts at a live cat hanging in a bag or a basket.

However, these barbaric habits were not practised universally. We should not forget the work of Francis of Assisi (1182–1226). He was the founder of the Franciscan order of monks and is also known for his love of and kindness towards all creatures: 'If you have men who will exclude any of God's creatures from the shelter of compassion and pity, you will have men who deal likewise with their fellow men.' Despite the papal bull stating that the devil took on the appearance of a cat, which was enough to condemn many to a dire end, a number of convents and monasteries still kept them. In 1500, the Jesuits landed in Quebec, bringing the first domestic cats to the North American continent.

THE MARTYRDOM OF CATS

Up to the 17th century, acts of cruelty towards cats were extremely barbaric. The illustration shows a pyre on the Place de Grève in Paris where cats were burned alive on the feast of Saint-Jean. (Illustration by Job, 1848–1931.)

One of the first official gestures of kindness shown towards cats is attributable to Louis XIV of France. In 1648, he banned the fire of Saint-Jean in the Place de Grève in Paris, stating that it was a 'barbaric and primitive tradition' to roast cats alive for the King's entertainment. And it was his minister, Colbert, who ordered the country's royal marines to keep two cats on board every ship to control vermin populations.

It was in England, at the start of the 18th century, that public opinion really started to change, eventually ending the systematic and organized killing of cats across Europe. Writers like Horace Walpole (1717–1797), author of *The Castle of Otranto*, and Daniel Defoe (1660–1731), author of *Robinson Crusoe*, began to make public their affection for the species. Defoe also noted that almost every family in London at this time owned at least one cat, which was treated with great respect. It was also during this period that scientist and mathematician Sir Isaac Newton (1642–1727) is said to have invented an early version of the catflap for his own pets.

In 1736, the Catholic Church, which was distancing itself more and more from its previous denouncement of cats (demonstrated by the fact that it was not unusual for clergymen to own them), abolished all laws that permitted sorcery trials against them.

Unfortunately, this change of heart came too late. The descendants of the cats who had survived several centuries of cruelty were not numerous or widespread enough to stop the grey rat from colonizing European towns. The large and aggressive wharf rat invaded Europe in 1750, and still infests some areas today. By the middle of the 18th century, however, the fortunes of cats had once again undergone a change. Now officially tolerated even by popes, they were finally no longer the hapless victims of religious persecution.

THE REHABILITATION OF THE CAT IN SOCIETY

In a society yearning for freedom, cats became a symbol of independence. Their regained popularity was assisted, in no small part, by the works of writers such as Lord Byron (1788–1824), Edgar Allan Poe (1809–1849), Charles Dickens (1812–70), Mark Twain (1835–1910), Henry James (1843–1916), Rudyard Kipling (1865–1936), William Butler Yeats (1865–1939) and T. S. Elliot (1888–1965). These writers portrayed the previously much-maligned cat as a creature of great mystery and beauty, demanding of respect and admiration. Poe, author of the chilling horror tale *The Black Cat*, the story of a cat that exacts revenge over its cruel and violent owner, expressed the wish that his tales might echo the mysterious nature of the cat. The all-knowing, uncompromising nature of the cat also caught the

THE PREDATOR
Cats finally began to be redeemed in the 18th century, when, as in Egyptian times, people acknowledged their usefulness as predators. (Fresco from the chapel of Saint Johannes, Austria.)

imagination of author Ernest Hemingway (1899–1961), who lived surrounded by six-toed (or polydactyl) cats in his home on Key West in the USA. 'A cat has absolute emotional honesty', he wrote. 'Human beings, for one reason or another, may hide their feelings, but a cat does not.' The cat's independence and air of mystery, which had once worked against it, made it the perfect subject for authors and poets in Europe and the Americas, endearing it to a generation and doing its bit to banish forgood the animal's previously bad reputation.

After centuries of persecution, the people of Great Britain were quick to take the cat into their hearts. In 1824, the Society for the Prevention of Cruelty to Animals (SPCA) was created, with backing from parliament. The society was the first law enforcement agency in the UK, and preceded the formation of the police force by five years. In 1840, Queen Victoria gave the royal seal of approval, and the organisation assumed the name it has kept ever since: The Royal Society for the Prevention of Cruelty to Animals (RSPCA). In 1871, the first-ever cat show took place at the Crystal Palace in London, presenting the cat as one of our best companions, and leading to the formation of the National Cat Club of Great Britain – the world's first cat club.

It is surprising that, after so many ups and downs, cats have not brought about any further controversy. The debate on the origins of cats, however, still puzzles the scientific world.

IN SEARCH OF THE COMMON CAT'S ANCESTORS

To seek out the origins of today's domesticated house cat, we need to dig back into the Earth's history many millions of years. The early mammals that arose from primitive insect-eating ancestors – such as the rat-sized Cretaceous Insectivore Procerberus (65–144 million years ago) – evolved to occupy the numerous ecological niches vacated by the wide extinctions of reptiles at the end of the Cretaceous period 65–70 million years ago.

Two groups of land-living placental mammals, the creodonts and the carnivores, became specialized meat-eaters. Opinion is divided as to whether the order Carnivora arose from the ancient creodonts or, as is now thought more likely, had a separate origin from the order Insectivora. Both orders of carnivorous mammals shared characteristic features: strong incisors for nipping; large canine teeth for stabbing; specialized cheek teeth for cutting and chewing meat (carnassials); strong jaws and sharp claws. When compared to the creodonts, the miacids, the common ancestors of all modern carnivores, were progressive in some very important features. They seem to have had a large and well-developed brain for their size, and their carnassial teeth, as in modern carnivores, included the fourth upper pre-molar and the first lower molar. These small weasel-like animals were probably forest-dwellers of the tropics.

THE LYNX

Some scientists believe that there are three species of lynx – one in North America, one in Europe and Asia, and one in Spain and Portugal. They have short tails and tufted ears.

The progressive miacids produced diverse lines 40 million years ago, which seem to have been the beginnings of the present-day families of Carnivora. Two major branches within the Carnivora were distinct by the late Eocene (38–55 million years ago) epoch. One branch, the superfamily Canoidea, today contains the families Canidae (dogs, wolves and foxes), Ursidae (bears), Ailuridae (pandas), Procyonidae (raccoons and coatis) and Mustelidae (weasels, martens, mink, wolverines and badgers), and gave rise to several families of marine carnivores (seals, sealions and walruses). The other branch, the Feloidea, now comprises the Felidae (cats) and the Viverridae (civets, hyenas and mongooses). The most primitive modern carnivores are some of the civets, little modified descendants of the progressive miacids. The viverrids may be considered to represent the basal stock of the feloid superfamily.

The separation of the first members of the cat family (Felidae) from their civet ancestors took place late in the Eocene. Once departed from the viverrid stem, the Felidae rapidly evolved into highly specialized animals. In the early Oligocene period, 30–34 million years ago, the first recognisable prototype cat (Proailurus) appeared. Pseudaelurus, a creature that is seen as the ancestor of all later cats, becomes apparent in the fossil record 16–20 million years ago. The subfamilies Machairodontinae and Felinae are both thought to derive from this animal.

The Felidae group contains two types of felines: the Pantherinae species, which are classified as big cats that can roar, but do not have a continuous purr (lions, leopards, tigers, jaguars and panthers); and the Felis species, which are cats and other small felines that purr but do not roar. In total, there are 36 species, which vary greatly in appearance and weight from 1.5 to 350 kilograms (3.3 to 770 pounds), but have a surprising number of anatomical similarities. For example, it can be seen at a glance that the tiny rusty-spotted cat (*see* p. 38) and the tiger belong to the same family.

There is only one feline that does not strictly belong in either of the two groups. This is the domestic cat (*Felis catus*), the pet cat that some specialists consider to be the 37th species. It is the most widely spread species – found in all continents except for Antarctica – and the most varied, comprising as many as 100 breeds.

ARE DOMESTIC CATS NOTHING MORE THAN TAMED WILD CATS?

Domestic and wild cats are basically alike. Most of the differences between the first domestic cats and wild cats – according to Charles Darwin's theories of evolution (1859) – can be explained as responses to changing environmental conditions. The smaller size of the domestic cat's skull, compared to most of its wild cousins, is a characteristic shared by all animals reared by humans. The more domesticated the animal, the smaller the brain. Domestic cats also have a longer digestive tract than their wild relatives, enabling them to digest the wider variety of food available to them in the civilized world. The more striking patterns and brighter colours of domestic cats' coats is evidence of the fact that camouflage is no longer a necessity for them.

Behavioural differences between wild and domestic cats are even more distinct. Adult domestic cats continue to show juvenile behaviour, such as purring, mewing for food and playing, whereas this behaviour disappears in 'tamed' wild cats as they reach maturity. Even when hand-reared, wild cats express their 'wildness' at the first opportunity they get by leaving home, just as they would have left their natural mother in the wild. Even when born in captivity from parents that are used to human beings, wild cats always remain on the look-out, and their fierce distrust of people distinguishes them from domestic cats. On the other hand, descendants of domestic cats that were tamed many thousands of years ago can either create a bond with their human owners or rediscover their innate wild instincts depending on their circumstances. If abandoned by its owner, a domestic cat will become feral, or wild, finding, unlike dogs, that its predatory instincts make independent survival possible.

DOMESTIC CATS AND THEIR PERSONALITIES

The body language used by pet cats speaks volumes, as does that used by their wild ancestors.

DOMESTIC CATS AND THEIR PERSONALITIES

INDIFFERENCE

DETERMINATION

GOOD MOOD

OPEN NESS

TOTAL JOY

CUNNING

RAGE

DISTRUST

UNHAPPINESS

JOY

LAZINESS

FLATTERY

Could it be said that the genetic mutations caused by the domestication of cats ended with the 37th species of Felidae? Advances in genetic research will probably give us an answer eventually. There are several different opinions today. Zoologists believe that animals that can breed from one generation to the next constitute a species. Therefore, the enforced hybridization of wild and domestic cats, rare in nature because breeds do not mix sexually, could indicate to which species of wild cat the domestic descendant belongs. The majority of animals born of these unions have not reproduced in their turn, but the domestic cat has recently been successfully hybridized with wild cats that are are currently considered to be a separate species, such as the serval (*Proailurus bengalensis*).

SO, WHO ARE THE TRUE ANCESTORS
OF DOMESTIC CATS?

The search for the ancestors of the domestic cat has not been a straightforward one, and has yet to be entirely resolved because we are still not certain of the origin of some sub-species of wild cat. However, a number of specialists now agree that European (including Scottish) and African wild cats and Asian steppe cats are members of the same polytypic species.

One might think that, because of the regions where cats have been domesticated, the part played by certain species of wild cat in the genetic heritage of different breeds of domestic cat would be significant. The Siamese cat, for example, is descended from non-pedigree Asian cats. One fact that has caused controversy for a long time is that female hybrids born of cross-breeding between wild and domestic cats were fertile, yet their offspring were sterile and not able to continue the line. A successful cross-breeding programme in the USA that resulted in the Bengal cat proved that hybridization was possible to some degree.

THE BENGALI CAT

Also known as the Chinese ocelot or leopard cat, the Bengali cat, according to some theories, could be one of the Siamese cat's ancestors.

Today, old methods of feline classification based on geography and anatomy, which led scientists to believe that our pet cats and the European forest cat were one and the same, have been abandoned.

The majority of specialists currently believe that the African wild cat (*Felis silvestris lybica*) is the main ancestor of our domestic cat, with the Asian steppe cat (*Felix silvestris ornata*), also known as the Indian desert cat, contributing to oriental breeds. This conclusion was arrived at after comparing their genetic imprints and skulls, and is supported by the fact that they are not as fierce as most wild cats, and could quite easily have been tamed.

It has also been observed that the Asian steppe cat's skull is similar to that of domestic cats. The naturalist Schauenberg believed that Asian steppe cats imported from Persia had bred with

African wild cats that had been 'tamed' by the Ancient Egyptians and that this is the origin of the domestic cat.

Domestic cats crossed the Mediterranean with the Phoenicians, the Roman legions and later with the Crusaders, and settled in Europe. They would have had occasional contact with the European forest cat, but the latter's contribution to the genetic heritage of our domestic cats seems to have been a minor one.

THREE OTHER SPECIES ARE CLOSELY RELATED TO THE DOMESTIC CAT

Nowadays, we can discern three separate species among the close relatives of the domestic cat. According to recent scientific theories, the Asian steppe cat (*Felis silvestris ornata*) is the main ancestor of the domestic cat, and is also a similar size. In general appearance it resembles the African wild cat, but its legs are shorter and its coat is usually mottled rather than striped.

There are about 12 varieties of African wild cat (*Felis silvestris Lybica*). These are found throughout Africa and the Middle East. Some experts believe that this species could easily be tamed, but others claim the opposite. The animal's tameability seems to depend on its living conditions and environment. According to genetic tests, hybridization between African wild cats and domestic cats is possible.

The European forest cat (*Felis silvestris silvestris*) is distinguishable by its thick fur marked with black stripes on the head and neck, making it look rather like a large tabby cat. In the past, it was hunted for its coat and was also killed because it was considered dangerous and was thought to be capable of attacking cattle. It is now a protected species, and several regional varieties survive in certain European countries. The European forest cat is wary of people, and is adept at climbing the trees amongst which it lives if it needs to take refuge. It is very shy which makes it practically impossible to tame, and any attempts to encourage it to breed with feral cats are usually unsuccessful. All the cats that have been produced from such matings have remained wild animals. European wild cats were once widespread throughout the UK, but became extinct outside Scotland in the 19th century due to loss of natural habitat and over-hunting. The Scottish wild cat has now been cut off from its ancestors for 8,000

MUMMY OF A CAT
African wild cats were 'tamed' by the Egyptians. When they died, their bodies were embalmed and then wrapped in bandages and placed inside a sarcophagus or a container of plaited straw. (Egyptian antiquities, Louvre Museum.)

years. The greatest current threat to wild cats throughout Europe is interbreeding with domestic cats, thus changing the animal's unique genetic make up for good.

SOME BREEDS OF DOMESTIC CAT COULD BE DESCENDED
FROM OTHER WILD SPECIES

In some places, other species of wild cat are believed to have contributed to the development of domestic breeds.

The chaus (*Felis chaus*) is the largest of all the domestic cat's close relatives. It can reach 1 metre (39 inches) in length (including the tail) and weighs approximately 15 kilograms (33 pounds). It is found in the jungles of Thailand and the Nile delta. In India, it interbred with domestic cats, and the resulting cross-breed was made to reproduce in captivity at London Zoo. Some researchers believe that, crossed with the African wild cat, the chaus could have engendered the first domestic cats reared by the Egyptians.

The manul (*Felis Manul*), or Pallas's cat is a small animal that weighs between 3 and 5 kilograms (6.6 and 11 pounds). It lives on the steppes and mountains of central Asia. Its long and exceptionally dense fur helps it to tolerate freezing temperatures, and it can be found at altitudes of up to 4,000 metres (13,100 feet). According to Pallas, the German naturalist after whom it is sometimes named, the manul could be the ancestor of the domestic Persian cat, but this theory has never been proved.

The sand cat (*Felis margarita*) lives in arid regions, from the deserts of Pakistan to the Sahara. It is sand coloured and weighs a maximum of 3 kilograms (6.6 pounds). It has thick tufts of fur between the pads of its feet, which allow it to walk on the sand without sinking. By day, it hides in burrows that it either digs for itself or borrows from other animals such as the fennec fox. *Felis thinobia* is considered to be an oriental sub-species of *Felis margarita*. It was discovered in the Transcaspian deserts, and was hybridized with domestic cats. According to some experts, this suggests that there is *thinobia* blood in the Persian lineage.

THE CAT IN EGYPT
The Ancient Egyptians considered their cats to be very important. Here, a cat is depicted in a wall painting found in the tomb of Menna in the Valley of the Nobles in Thebes.

The black footed cat (*Felis nigripes*) is the smallest cat in Africa. When fully grown, it weighs less than 2.5 kilograms (5.5 pounds). It closely resembles the Sahara sand cat, but has a darker coat and, as its name suggests, black paws. In captivity, it can be cross-bred with domestic cats.

The Bengali cat (*Prionailurus bengaleusis*), also known as the leopard cat, has an immense area of distribution: from Manchuria to the Indo-Malay regions, and from Pakistan to China. By cross-breeding with cats from the *Lybica-ornata* group, it became the stock of the Siamese breed. Crossed with a female American Shorthair in 1963, this cat gave birth to the Bengal, which is now considered to be one of the most beautiful domestic breeds.

The serval (*Felis serval*) lives in the savannahs. It is a good swimmer, and is often found near lakes and rivers. It weighs approximately 15 kilograms (33 pounds). It has long, strong legs that allow it to leap after birds and catch them in flight. In the USA, breeders have recently managed to cross-breed a serval with a Havana Brown – a domestic breed related to Siamese and black European cats – and have created a new breed called Savannah. This large cat, which is still very rare, has apparently not inherited the wild nature of the serval and is actually very tame.

CATS THAT ARE GEOGRAPHICALLY AND PHYSICALLY DISTINCT CAN SHARE THE SAME DNA

In order to clearly define their origin and their contribution to feline evolution, the genetic imprints of each species must be studied. This has yet to be accomplished, and there are sure to be more surprises in store. It was recently discovered that cats that are geographically and physically very distinct can share the same DNA. But for now, we should think of the species described below as the cousins, not the ancestors, of the domestic cat.

The African golden cat (*Profelis aurata*) is quite rare and not much studied. It dwells in the African forest massifs, where it feeds on small mammals and birds. It weighs between 13 and 18 kilograms (28 and 40 pounds) and has a magnificent dark golden coat.

The caracal (*Caracal caracal*) is a medium-sized cat with very long ears and pale-tipped fur. It lives on dry, open land in parts of Africa, Asia and the Middle East, where it comes out at night to feed on birds and other small animals.

The fishing cat (*Prionailurus viverrina*) has short, slightly webbed paws and is not able to retract its claws easily. It has adapted to suit its environment – the marshlands, mangrove swamps and estuaries of tropical Asia – where it lives on a diet of frogs, snakes and fish.

THE CARACAL

According to some writers, caracals were used in the past, like cheetahs, to hunt hares and birds.

The tiny flat-headed cat (*Felis planiceps*) gets its name from the flattened dome shape of its skull. It has a long snout, which is why it is sometimes called the weasel cat, and its ears are positioned at the sides of its head. It weighs a maximum of 2 kilograms (4.4 pounds), and lives in humid parts of Malaysia, Borneo and Sumatra. Its claws, like those of the cheetah, are not retractable, and it uses them to harpoon fish, frogs and crustaceans.

The rusty-spotted (*Felis rubiginosus*), or rust-patched, cat has a grey or brown coat covered with rust-coloured markings. It weighs no more than 1 or 2 kilograms (2.2 or 4.4 pounds), measures just over 40 centimetres (16 inches) long and is the most beautiful of the small felines. It lives in southern Indian and Sri Lankan scrublands. According to some, it can be domesticated if captured young.

The Chinese desert cat (*Felis bieti*) is rare and virtually unknown. It is the same size as a large domestic cat and lives on the borders of China and Mongolia up to a height of 3,000 metres (9,840 feet). Its coat, which is yellow-brown in colour, blends in with its surroundings.

The iriomote cat (*Felis iriomotensis*) was discovered in 1967 on the small island of Iriomote in the archipelago of Ryuku, Japan. There are only about 100 of these cats alive today.

THE DOMESTIC CAT DID NOT REACH THE AMERICAN CONTINENT UNTIL THE 16TH AND 17TH CENTURIES

North America became detached from Eurasia eight to 12 million years ago. The feline species that lived in North America at this time evolved in different ways, and then spread to South America when this continent rejoined its northern counterpart. It was only when the Americas were colonized by humans that domestic cats arrived there in any number. By this time, the American continent was inhabited by several species of wild cats.

The puma (*Puma concolor*), or cougar, purrs and has a silhouette similar to that of a big cat. Although it does not attack humans, it can be a threat for other reasons. It is a skilled deer-hunter, and will also attack domestic cattle if given the opportunity.

The ocelot (*Leopardus pardalis*) is similar in size to the lynx and weighs approximately 15 kilograms (33 pounds). It was once widespread in the southern states of North America and in the north of Argentina. Its beautiful, silver highlighted coat is highly coveted, and trade in it once threatened the species with extinction. It has been protected by the Washington Convention since 1989, but it is still not completely out of danger. Although it is illegal to hunt this animal, some poachers are willing to risk breaking the law.

FELIS CONCOLOR OR PUMA

Commonly called the puma or cougar, this is the largest member of the Felis family. Its muscly body can measure up to 1.5 metres (5 feet) long and weigh up to 100 kilograms (220 pounds).

The margay (*Leopardus wiedi*) can be found from Mexico to Argentina, where it is sought after for its beautiful coat. Although officially protected, this animal has disappeared from many areas. The margay is about the same size as a large domestic cat and weighs between 4 and 9 kilograms (8.8 and 20 pounds). It is extremely agile and spends most of its time in the trees. It is the only cat that can go down a tree head first!

The pampas cat, or colocolo, (*Oncifelis colocolo*) lives between Ecuador and Patagonia. Its coveted coat camouflages it in the grass at night, where it hunts rodents and birds that have nested on the ground.

Geoffroy's cat (*Oncifelis geoffroyi*) lives between Brazil and Argentina. It spends most of its time in the trees, where it shows great climbing skills. It is also said to be an excellent swimmer.

It gets its name from the French naturalist Geoffroy Saint-Hilaire (pioneer in embryology and creator of the Paris botanical gardens), who discovered it in the 19th century.

The tiger cat, or oncilla, (*Leopardus tigrinus*) looks like a miniature ocelot, and weighs between 2 and 3 kilograms (4.4 to 6.6 pounds). It lives only in the Central American forest in the north of Argentina. It was once a victim of its own beauty, but is now a protected species and is slowly recovering.

The jaguarondi (*Herpailurus yagouaroundi*) is a strange animal about which little is known. It has an elongated body, which measures about 0.5 metres (18 inches), and weighs around 12 kilograms (26 pounds). With its short legs, the jaguarondi looks like a large weasel with a mongoose's head.

The kodkod (*Onciferis guigna*) is the lightest of the American felines, weighing less than 3 kilograms (6.6 pounds) and is found in Chile and Argentina. It climbs into trees when it is threatened, where its patched, dark-ochre coat makes it hard to spot amongst the foliage.

MODERN BREEDS OF CAT

There are believed to be approximately 400 million cats alive in the world today. The majority of these are domestic cats (7.7 million in the United Kingdom) and stray cats (eight to ten million in the United Kingdom). There are also several hundred thousand wild cats, a number of species of which are in danger of extinction.

In the 18th century, there were only four known breeds of domestic cat, and all of them were products of natural selection: the domestic cat, the angora cat, the Spanish cat and the French Chartreux cat. A century later, another four breeds, which also evolved naturally, were added to the list: a Chinese breed with droopy ears (which has now disappeared), two short-tailed breeds (a Malay one resembling the Siamese cat, and a Japanese one similar to the Japanese Bobtail), and a cat with no tail at all – today's Manx. At the beginning of the 20th century, two important new breeds were reared in Britain: the Persian and the Abyssinian. Recent research suggests that there are now 12 naturally evolved breeds: Turkish Angora, Turkish Van, Maine Coon, Norwegian Forest, Siberian Forest, Manx, Japanese Bobtail, American Shorthair, Chartreux, Korat, Siamese and Burmese.

THE JAGUARONDI

In the past, native Americans used the jaguarondi to control the spread of rodents.

The world's first cat show, in London in 1871, set the trend for pedigree cats. From 1900 onwards, the domestic cat species continued to acquire new breeds, which came mainly from British breeders. There are now approximately 100 breeds of domestic cat.

Some breeds have appeared spontaneously among communities of cats living in

geographically isolated areas. Over time, natural selection fixes certain characteristics and eliminates others. Members of the same feline community, therefore, may develop a psychological and physical uniformity, which accords with the notion of a breed. This is the case with Siamese, Chartreux, European Shorthair, Norwegian Forest, Maine Coon and Singapura cats. This natural selection process can also aid the creation of different coat types, as with the colourpoint pattern of Siamese cats and the blue coat of the Chartreux.

Natural mutations may also be at the root of a breed or variety. One can therefore cross-breed cats with similar mutations, increasing their numbers and, at the same time, diversifying their origins in order to avoid the problems associated with inbreeding. This is how the Scottish Fold and Sphinx breeds were created, as well as the Chinchilla and Golden Persian varieties. The majority of breeds and varieties, however, have been created by cross-breeding and artificial selection. The Persian cat, for example, originated from cross-breeding between an Angora and an English cat of the European type. It is not sufficient, however, simply to encourage mating between different subjects in the hope of creating a new breed or variety. Knowledge of genetics is essential, and several generations have to be produced before the results of the match become apparent.

THE CAT'S PLACE IN THE 21ST CENTURY

Of all the cat species, the domestic cat may be the only one that need not fear the progress of human civilisation. The more urban our societies become, the better settled cats become. In the USA, domestic cats have outnumbered dogs since the beginning of the 1980s. This is due, not only to the fertility of the species (the family descended from one female cat can extend to as many as 20,000 kittens in just five years), but also to their resistance and ability to adapt. Unlike pedigree cats, which represent only about eight per cent of the cat population in the United Kingdom, non-pedigree cats have a bright future ahead of them: they have been around for years and their birth-rate will never be totally under control.

The conditions of modern city life play an important role in the integration of cats. Increasing numbers of people are living alone (due to longer life-expectancy, divorce etc.) and pet animals can reduce stress and provide companionship. Cats win points over dogs because they do not need taking out regularly and do not want their owners to spend all their time with them. They are usually less noisy and are also cheaper to keep than dogs. Apart from the advantage of being generally lower maintenance than dogs, cats can also be useful, and are valued for their rat- and mouse-catching skills. Above all, cats are kept today for their beauty and grace and for the companionship they provide. Although undoubtedly independent of spirit, many cats do value their owner's company – they just may not always show it.

LOOK

CATS HAVE AN IRRITATING HABIT OF TURNING THEIR BACKS ON YOU,
BUT SOME WILL POSE QUITE NICELY. HERE IS A COLLECTION OF A FEW
CATS OUT-AND-ABOUT – BEING INQUISITIVE, STRETCHING AND
JUMPING – BUT MOSTLY JUST RELAXING OF COURSE!

And lifts to the changing moon, His changing eyes.

William Butler Yeats, **The Cat and the Moon.**

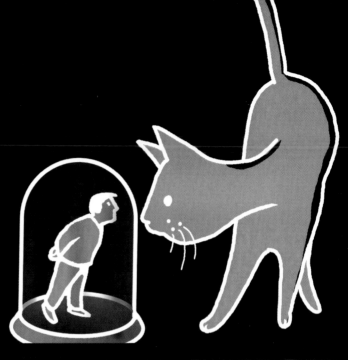

IN PRACTICE

CATS ARE DOMESTIC ANIMALS THAT ARE HAPPY TO SHARE OUR LIVES,
THOUGH THEIR WILDER INSTINCTS ARE NEVER FAR FROM THE SURFACE.
AS EVERY CAT-LOVER KNOWS, CATS ARE FAR FROM INSCRUTABLE, AND THE
ANGLE OF A TAIL, THE TONE OF A MIAOW, AND EVEN A FACIAL EXPRESSION,
CAN SPEAK VOLUMES. LIVING WITH A CAT, AND LEARNING TO UNDERSTAND
AND RESPECT IT, IS THE BEST WAY TO GET TO KNOW ONE BETTER.

How much does a cat cost?

Generally speaking, cats are not very expensive to keep. Apart from food, and possibly cat litter, you are only likely to have to budget for veterinary expenses, which will vary depending on your cat's health.

Transport

Your basket or carrying box should be well-ventilated, and large enough for your cat to stand, sit and turn around in easily. Cover the bottom of the box or basket with a thick layer of kitchen roll or newspaper, in order to avoid untimely leaks. Make sure that you have a couple of small containers with you so that you can offer your cat a drink. On lengthy trips, something to eat may be considered. If you are travelling by public transport, you may have to pay a fare for your pet (see page 110).

Buying a cat

A pedigree kitten costs between about £250 and £500, depending on its breed and any titles won by its parents in shows. Cats can also be purchased through animal protection societies, where a donation of between £40 and £60 will be expected, to cover the costs of vaccination, neutering and often microchipping. Small ads posted by individuals are often displayed in veterinary surgeries. It is a good idea to seek advice before buying a pedigree cat, so that you are aware of any special care requirements and to enable you to choose a breed that is suitable for your lifestyle and location.

The journey home

Thanks to their size, cats are easy to transport – but they don't exactly enjoy travelling. If your journey is a long one, especially by public transport, a mild sedative can be obtained under veterinary supervision. However, the effects of these drugs are unpredictable and their use is not recommended unless your cat is a very nervous traveller. Inform your vet if extreme temperatures are likely to be encountered en route – commonly used sedatives can affect your cat's 'thermostat'. Give your cat a light meal before you set off.

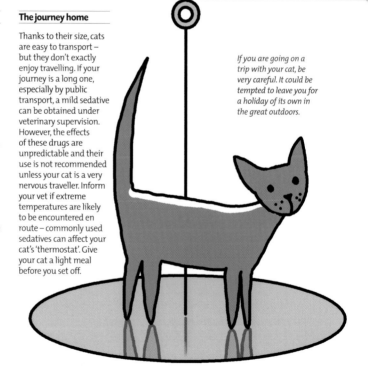

If you are going on a trip with your cat, be very careful. It could be tempted to leave you for a holiday of its own in the great outdoors.

Food budget

A 4-kilogram (8.8-pound) cat will eat at least 200 grams (7 ounces) of moist food, or 90 grams (3.15 ounces) of dry food, each day. A 400-gram (14-ounce) tin of medium-quality food costs between 50 pence and 80 pence, and a 400-gram (14-ounce) box of dry food of the same quality is about 80 pence. The cost per day, therefore, comes to between 25 pence and 40 pence for tinned moist food and approximately 16 pence for dry food. If calculated on an annual basis, cat food costs a minimum of about £60 and a maximum of about £150. Processed food, especially dry food, is certainly cheaper than home-cooking with fresh meat or fish. Cats can be fed your leftovers but, where possible, it is best to alternate these with food that meets feline nutrition requirements. If you use cat litter, a 5-kilogram (11-pound) bag will cost about £1.50. If you use one bag a week, then you will spend about £78 on litter each year.

Health budget

Vaccines, neutering, identity-chipping, worming and flea treatments are possible health costs. Vets do not have a national pricing structure, and fees vary depending on the type of practice and its location. The first expenses arise with the primary vaccinations (against 'cat 'flu', feline infectious enteritis and feline leukemia) at nine and twelve weeks, which cost £40–£65. The yearly booster costs £20–£35. Castration of males is in the region of £20–£45 and spaying of females £30–£60. Cats Protection does, however, sometimes offer neutering vouchers for those in need. Microchipping costs £20–£30. Clinics at veterinary schools and charity-run surgeries often charge less than other places.

Alternate processed food with family leftovers. These are just as good for your purse as for your moggie!

Change your cat's litter several times a week. Forgetting to do so is unhygienic, and the cat would have no qualms about using your sofa instead if it didn't fancy the litter tray.

HEALTH INSURANCE

There are several companies that offer insurance policies for pets, covering risks such as illness, accidents, hospitalisation and surgery. But these policies often have restrictions concerning the age of the cat, excess payments, compulsory vaccinations etc. You should examine these policies carefully before you take one out. As with other insurance, the costs of each claim are not totally refunded.

A cat's territory

Sleeping, playing and eating are a cat's main occupations. It spends about two-thirds of its life either sleeping or dozing. If it can go outside, it will spend up to four hours each day hunting and playing and, if kept indoors, it will spend the same amount of time doing things like playing with its owners, mooching about or gazing out of the window. Both indoor and outdoor cats dedicate another four hours a day to grooming. They spend 15 minutes a day eating, broken into several sessions. Cats love to nibble and, if you give them the chance, they will eat up to 15 small meals in a 24-hour period.

Cruel or calming?

Cats are often frowned upon for playing with their prey, either before killing it or afterwards. But there is no cruelty (in the human sense of the word) in this activity. It has been observed that this behaviour lasts longer if the cat has worked long and hard to capture its prey, which indicates that it may be linked to tension, or even fear felt by the cat during the chase. Perhaps playing with their prey in this way helps cats to relax before they start eating.

Cat's play

From the age of three weeks, kittens start to play with their brothers and sisters or their mother. These games usually involve one or more kittens – they roll about on the floor, turn their bellies up, arch their backs, stand on their hind legs in a boxing stance, chase and stalk. Through these different gymnastic sequences, cats build their personalities and develop the skills and reflexes that they will use in adulthood. At about four or five weeks old, a kitten will start to play alone, first chasing its mother's tail and then running after small objects. It may, for example, pat a ball and push it along, before catching it between its paws ... and then start again. Such games are not reserved for kittens however – many adult domestic cats behave in the same way.

When in a flat, a cat will behave in the same way as it does outdoors, adapting to the reduced space at its disposal.

It is important that your cat has its meals in a corner far away from its litter tray. If you have two cats it is best to have one litter tray for each.

...you have two cats, it is essential to ...t them choose their own sleeping ...aces; if you do not respect their ...oices they may fight.

A cat sees its owner as part of its territory, which is why it will leave its scent by rubbing against your legs. Cats do not give their trust easily, but when they do it lasts forever. They can be totally loyal, and often show clear signs of jealousy if anyone, human or animal, distracts their owner's attention. However, a cat only shows affection when it is in the mood and will never give up its natural independence.

A cat's social behaviour

Cats are naturally solitary animals. Unlike many other species, their social organisation allows them to avoid conflicts with cats they do not wish to dominate. In the wild, cats take on a domain, which they divide into several areas for specific uses, such as resting, hunting, reproducing, playing and eating. Any owner will be familiar with the cat's tendency to mark its territory by urinating. But it is less commonly known that cats leave other smells, secreted by glands situated mainly on either side of their heads and tails. They rub their bodies against objects such as trees and furniture to mark them with their scent, and may also leave visible marks such as scratches. An intruder daring to violate another cat's territory will not necessarily be attacked. If the resident cat has seen it from afar, it may take the opportunity to distance itself. On the other hand, if surprised or cornered, a cat will assume different postures and mew or growl defensively to warn off its opponent before resorting to fighting.

The hunting instinct

The impulse to hunt is always present in cats. While dogs live in a world dominated by hearing and, above all, smell, vision is a priority for cats. When a cat sees potential prey moving, its wilder instincts rise to the surface, and it will inevitably begin to hunt.

Breeds and characteristics

Members of each breed have the same physical features and, to a certain extent, the same kind of character.

Cats are extremely sensitive to their environment, so the conditions under which they are reared and the personalities of their parents and owners are likely to influence their character. Within the same breed, some cats can have a more marked temperament than others. Breeds are divided into three main types, according to their basic shape.

'Chatty' cats

Being vocal, or chatty, is a typically oriental trait, mainly associated with Siamese cats. These cats hate to be ignored, and communicate with their owners by constantly mewing.

Cuddly cats

French Chartreux, Birman, Maine Coon and Ragdoll cats are peaceful and always ready to be stroked. Some, like the Turkish Angora, Balinese and Bombay, stick to their owners like glue and will not let them out of their sight. This is also true of the most playful of breeds, the Singapura.

Private cats

These cats do not like to have their habits disturbed. They include Persians, Abyssinians, Russian Blues and Manx.

Adventurous cats

These cats are naturally independent. They are descended from non-pedigree cats, and include breeds such as European or American Shorthairs, the tailless Japanese Bobtail and the curly-coated Cornish Rex.

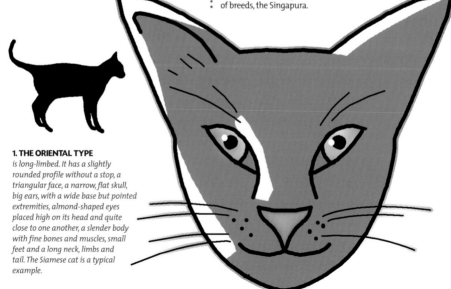

1. THE ORIENTAL TYPE
is long-limbed. It has a slightly rounded profile without a stop, a triangular face, a narrow, flat skull, big ears, with a wide base but pointed extremities, almond-shaped eyes placed high on its head and quite close to one another, a slender body with fine bones and muscles, small feet and a long neck, limbs and tail. The Siamese cat is a typical example.

2. THE EUROPEAN TYPE

is a medium-limbed cat. It has a rectilinear profile and not a very prominent stop. Face on, its head is trapeze-shaped with a large, rounded forehead. It has slightly almond-shaped eyes, a well-defined, muscular body and solid limbs. The European is a typical example.

3. THE PERSIAN TYPE

is short-limbed. It has a marked stop and a short nose, a round head (face on), a large skull and a rounded forehead. It has small ears, which are rounded at the tips, placed low on its head and spaced well apart. It has a sturdy body, compact musculature, strong bones and large round paws. The Persian is a typical example.

The language of cats

When not mating or carrying young, cats tend to communicate with each other from a distance – this allows them to show their disapproval yet avoid confrontation. With people, they usually adopt a friendlier tone. This does not stop them from scratching us from time to time when we fail to spot the signs of impatience they show before lashing out.

DEFENSIVE AND READY TO ATTACK

Ears pointing backwards, whiskers sticking out to the sides, slightly closed eyes and open mouth: this posture shows two intentions: the cat is both on the defensive and ready to attack.

TOTAL CONFIDENCE

Eyes wide open, straight ears pointing slightly forwards – one possibly towards a noise, lips resting: the cat is confident and attentive to things going on around it.

Facial expressions

Cats involve us in their emotions using their whiskers, their ears (which they can move independently and in all directions), their eyes, and even by wrinkling their foreheads. Their faces are versatile and capable of showing a range of different feelings, or suddenly changing expression.

Voices

Up to the age of five weeks, cats have a limited vocal range, but they develop their full repertoire of sounds between the sixth and eighth months of life. Many of these sounds will be used mainly to communicate with people. Cats are naturally solitary animals, so to who else would they insistently say 'Meow, I'm hungry'? Who else would they greet with a sweet purr-like mewing? Cats have 60 or more sounds reserved only for contact with people. When confronting each other or when mating, cats usually cry, growl or snarl, using a deeper pitch than they would normally use with us.

Purring

Is a purring cat a happy cat? Recent studies of the purring mechanism have revealed that this is not always the case. Purring sounds are produced when the larynx vibrates continuously, which is caused by the cat breathing in and out. A kitten starts to purr with its mother when it is two days old, indicating when it is hungry, content or in need of maternal contact. Adult domestic cats continue to use this method of communication with their owners, but non-socialised adult stray cats do not seem to purr. Purring is not an automatic reflex action, which explains why some pet cats rarely purr, or do not purr at all. As well as being an expression of contentment, cats may also purr when they are sick or unhappy. In these cases, it probably means that the cat is just feeling ill at ease with its surroundings.

ON THE DEFENSIVE
Ears flattened out to the sides, forehead rounded, whiskers flattened sideways, the eyes are half closed and the canines showing: the cat is frightened and ready to defend itself.

Body language

A cat's posture and body language, if you pay attention to them, can tell you a lot about its condition, mood and attitude towards its surroundings. Here are a few examples to help you to understand them.

The position of a cat's tail plays an important role in its body language. The tail is always concave or lowered when a cat assumes a threatening posture. On the other hand, a horizontal tail can be a sign of both happiness and unhappiness – the difference between which is undoubtedly clear to cats. Similarly, when a cat, faced with another cat, lies on its back with its paws in the air and its ears flattened out to the sides, it does not show submission, but warns of imminent confrontation.

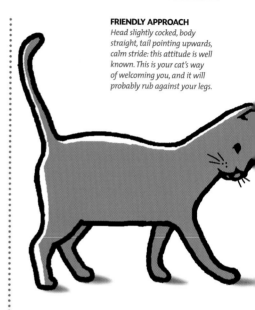

FRIENDLY APPROACH
Head slightly cocked, body straight, tail pointing upwards, calm stride: this attitude is well known. This is your cat's way of welcoming you, and it will probably rub against your legs.

INVITATION TO PLAY OR STROKE
If your cat suddenly lies on its back with its paws facing upwards it is asking you to play with it or give it a cuddle.

THE MENACING POSTURE, CLOSE AND OFFENSIVE

Strange attitude of two cats sitting facing each other. Their bodies are relaxed but they are ready to confront each other. Their gestures indicate an imminent conflict, which will start with little movements of the paws and will develop into a fight.

THE STALKER'S POSITION

Cats often use this posture for hunting, but also while playing. It is intriguing to watch. The cat will concentrate on a movement that seems invisible to us, holding its breath, lifting its posterior and waggling it once or twice before leaping.

THE DEFENSIVE, MENACING POSITION

A cat will try to impress an adversary from a distance by making itself look larger than it really is, while walking backwards and making its escape. This is often accompanied by noisy growls.

The five senses

Pet cats do not use their fantastic senses to the full. However, if they are left to survive in the great outdoors, they have to depend on their sharp eyesight, acute hearing, strong sense of smell and tactile faculties.

Cats' sense of touch is already present and well-developed at birth. Their whole bodies are sensitive, but their paws and whiskers are especially useful for exploring their surroundings. The long, stiff hairs that form the whiskers and eyebrows have a mass of nerves at their base and work like antennae. Thanks to these, cats can determine the position of their limbs in space and move around in the dark without bumping into things.

HEARING
In kittens, the part of the brain that analyses sounds starts to function two or three days after birth. Cats have much sharper hearing than humans. We pick up 20,000 Hz (vibrations per second), but cats can hear at least two to three times more. This sharp hearing is due to a marked development of the ear drum, accompanied by the ability to isolate one sound from another. Thanks to the mobility of their outer ears, cats can locate a distant sound to within a few centimetres.

TASTE
When a kitten is ten days old, it can already differentiate the four basic tastes: saltiness, sweetness, bitterness and acidity. The taste buds are in the foliated parts of the tongue, so if a cat loses its sense of smell, it will also lose its sense of taste. Cats usually prefer bitter, acid and salty tastes and they really 'savour' water because they have specific taste organs that enable them to appreciate the quality and the taste of water.

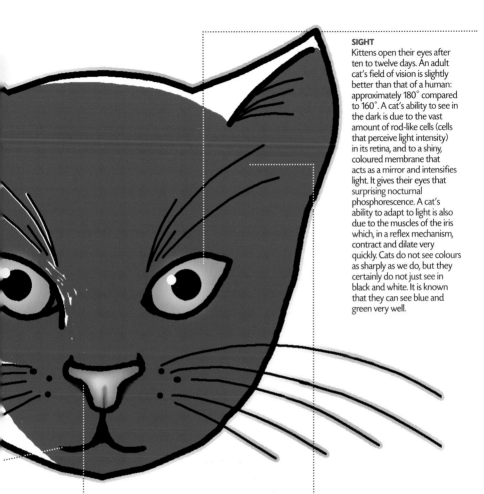

SIGHT

Kittens open their eyes after ten to twelve days. An adult cat's field of vision is slightly better than that of a human: approximately 180° compared to 160°. A cat's ability to see in the dark is due to the vast amount of rod-like cells (cells that perceive light intensity) in its retina, and to a shiny, coloured membrane that acts as a mirror and intensifies light. It gives their eyes that surprising nocturnal phosphorescence. A cat's ability to adapt to light is also due to the muscles of the iris which, in a reflex mechanism, contract and dilate very quickly. Cats do not see colours as sharply as we do, but they certainly do not just see in black and white. It is known that they can see blue and green very well.

SMELL

It is well-known that the sense of smell is particularly important for cats. From the third day after birth, the kitten chooses one of its mother's teats, which it can recognise by its smell. Cats have about 200 million olfactory cells, whereas humans have only five million. The nose is linked to the roof of the mouth and it plays a particularly important role, amongst other things, allowing the male to pick up sexual pheromones. These are chemical substances secreted and released for detection and response by another animal, produced by the female on heat.

BALANCE

Towards the 40th day, a kitten will already be able to land on all fours after a jump or a fall. But it is possible for a cat to fall badly, especially if it falls vertically or head first: it all depends on the height of the fall and on the position the cat is in when it starts to fall.

Unceremonious love

Feline love affairs are tumultuous and noisy. The sexual instinct is strong in domestic animals, and you might even have to cope with sexual hyperactivity, which can often be accompanied by aggression.

In the UK, about 70 per cent of male and 80 per cent of female pet cats have been neutered, and will be pretty much oblivious to the mating season. However, for unneutered cats, sex is a major behavioural drive. The mating season draws males out of the isolation in which they like to dwell, to seek out the presence of a female cat. However, the absence of female company may make a male search for a substitute, which can sometimes be another male. A female in season secretes strong scents to attract the male – these are known as pheromones. She calls to the male in a loud and plaintive voice, rolls around on the ground, and rubs up against legs and other objects, holding her rear end high with her tail upright. A male cat living in semi-freedom will sometimes disappear for several days chasing after a female, or queen. He will often return in a pitiful state, after savage battles fought in the attempt to win over the female of his desires.

Temporary contraception

This can be used only for female cats, and it consists of two chemical methods (a pill or an injection) and a physical one. The pill has to be given before the female comes into season or, at the latest, when the first signs appear, as it suppresses the current cycle. An injection will block the cycle for five to eight months. For advice about physical contraception, which involves artificially stimulating ovulation, speak to your vet. Contraception can be used only in genitally healthy females, and it should be suspended from time to time to allow for the return of normal oestrus.

Castration and spaying

These methods of contraception are irreversible. In males, castration should be carried out when the cat is six to nine months old. It involves removing the testicles under general anaesthetic, and the cat can be taken home the same evening. In females, spaying usually takes place at six months of age, avoiding the first oestrus period. The removal of the ovaries and uterus is carried out under general anaesthetic. The cat is usually discharged the same evening and its stitches can be removed ten to 14 days later. Male cats neutered before puberty are less likely to spray, wander or get into fights, and the operation does not cause any psychological problems.

Reproduction

Thousands of cats are abandoned every year. You should not let nature take its course unless you are sure you can find a family for all the kittens. Only then can you prepare yourself for the pleasure of watching them grow.

The right time for mating

The age at which puberty is reached depends on breed and type. Most males reach sexual maturity by nine to ten months, and most females have their first oestrus at six to seven months, although it is better for their health if they do not have any kittens before they are at least a year old. Mating is usually timed so that kittening avoids the depths of winter, but with some breeds (e.g. Siamese) it can take place at any time of the year – sometimes occurring every month. As for males, the mere presence of a female in season is enough to excite them. If you want pedigree kittens, approach someone who breeds cats of the same breed as yours to choose an animal of the opposite sex. You will probably have to pay the owner of the male cat. Sexual intercourse between cats is brief, noisy and often repeated.

When can you tell whether mating has been successful?

Foetuses can be felt through palpation of the abdomen from the 20th day, but the formal diagnosis is made at one month. By then, the foetuses are quite well developed, the mother's belly is rounded and her nipples are swollen. Pregnancy lasts between 58 and 70 days. In the final stages, the cat may become agitated and will start searching for the best place to give birth. You should help her by placing a large basket with clean material in it in a quiet, private place that she seems to like.

The process of giving birth

The first contractions are barely noticeable. The cat will not be able to keep still and will constantly lick her genitalia. More than an hour and a half can pass before the first kitten appears. The mother will tear the amniotic sac protecting the kitten and clean its face so that it can breathe. She will then cut the umbilical cord and eat the placenta. The interval between one kitten and the next is usually about half an hour, but it can vary. An average litter will contain three to five kittens.

Cats make good mothers and dedicate themselves completely to their kittens, leaving them only from time to time to feed. They will even adopt another cat's young if necessary.

When should you call the vet?

A cat may send out a plea for help by settling down near her owner when the first kitten is about to be born. Giving birth is normally uneventful, but there are certain situations when you will need to contact a veterinary surgeon – if the cat does not give birth after her waters have broken (particularly if there is a greenish discharge), if she stops pushing in labour, if a kitten remains stuck at the entrance of the vulva, if there is significant blood loss, or if the cat is several days late in giving birth.

A balanced diet

Cats are carnivores, but we have transformed them into semi-omnivores, feeding them anything from scraps of cheese to chocolate. But it is important not to ignore their preferences and nutritional requirements. Their bodies need certain foods in order to function properly.

A fully grown pet cat weighing 3 kilograms (6.6 pounds) needs 210 calories a day, but one of the same weight that gets extra exercise will need 270 calories. As a rule, you should start with 70 to 90 calories and multiply this by the weight of the cat in kilograms. There are two exceptions to this rule – for heavily pregnant cats, multiply the calories by 1.5, and for nursing mothers, multiply them by three. All cats are different, and allowing your pet to over-eat will lead to obesity, which can cause serious health problems.

Mineral glucides + vitamins + proteins + lipids.

Undiluted milk is the best source of calcium and phosphorus, but it can cause diarrhoea in some cats if given in large quantities.

Choosing the right food

Raw egg yolks provide excellent nutrition for kittens because they contain vitamin A and proteins. Egg whites, on the other hand, contain an enzyme that degrades the vitamin biotin, a substance necessary for growth and for healthy skin, hair and nails. An egg yolk can be mixed into food once or twice a week.

Meat and fish

Choose slightly fatty pieces of beef, lamb, chicken, turkey or veal. Serve red meat raw or lightly grilled (when overcooked it loses 60 per cent of its vitamins). White meat should be cooked to avoid the possibility of bacterial food poisoning. The best fish are coley and cod. Oily fish, such as sardines and herrings, should be fed only as a treat. Fish contains less protein than meat, so a portion of fish should be larger than one of meat. The fish should be cooked and boned. Offal (liver, heart, etc.) has a high nutritional value, but lungs do not, although they may be suitable for an obese cat. Rich offal should be given only once a week because it contains too much vitamin A, and it must always be cooked or it may cause diarrhoea. Mature cheese is rich in calcium and is recommended during growth, pregnancy and lactation. It is also suitable for cats that are suffering from immobility or arthritis.

Vegetables and cereals

Cereals, especially rice and oat flakes, can be included in a cat's diet. Rice must be cooked until it becomes paste-like. Vegetables, such as spinach, lettuce, green beans and carrots, help bowel movements and are low in calories. They are always recommended for slimming diets and should be well cooked so that they are easy to digest.

CALORIES

For 100 grams (3.5 ounces)

Beef (lean):	150 Kcal
Lamb (lean):	130 Kcal
Chicken (breast):	120 Kcal
Ox heart:	125 Kcal
Ox liver:	150 Kcal
Cow's milk:	65 Kcal
Egg:	160 Kcal
Whiting:	70 Kcal
Mackerel:	130 Kcal
Cooked rice:	120 Kcal
Cooked carrots:	30 Kcal

PRACTICAL TIPS

Mix ingredients together, so that your cat eats everything in its dish. Always leave a bowl of water available, and change it twice a day. Wash your cat's dishes every day and rinse them to get rid of any traces of washing-up liquid, making sure you keep them separate from your own dishes. Do not change your cat's diet suddenly – alternate new and old foods for at least a week. Pulses, cabbage, pork, sauces, spices and onions are not recommended. The nutritional requirements of older cats change, and they may have to follow a diet recommended by a vet. The easiest way to ensure that your cat gets a balanced diet is to give it a prepared food from a reputable company. Check that the one you choose is intended for maintenance and not just for snacking.

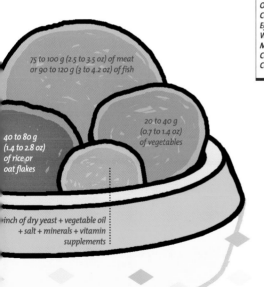

75 to 100 g (2.5 to 3.5 oz) of meat or 90 to 120 g (3 to 4.2 oz) of fish

20 to 40 g (0.7 to 1.4 oz) of vegetables

40 to 80 g (1.4 to 2.8 oz) of rice or oat flakes

•inch of dry yeast + vegetable oil + salt + minerals + vitamin supplements

First-aid at home

Almost no cat, however tame, will accept medical care without a battle. The right approach can make your job much easier.

1. RESTRAINING A CAT
To avoid being scratched, spread a towel on a table, pick your cat up by the scruff of its neck and put it on the towel. Hold the cat close to the table by gently pushing down and, without letting go of the scruff, wrap it in the towel.

2. OPENING THE MOUTH
Place your thumb and fore finger at either side of your cat's jaw and squeeze gently. At the same time, tilt the head back and press carefully on the tip of the lower jaw, with the index finger of your other hand.

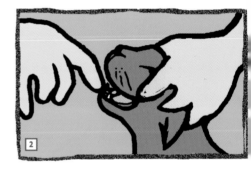

3. PUTTING DROPS IN THE EARS
Sit or stand to one side of your cat, hold its head firmly and gently fold back the ear flap while you apply the drops. Then massage the base of the ear to help the drops to penetrate.

4. APPLYING BANDAGES
Disinfect the wound, cover it with gauze and wrap an elastic bandage around the injured area. Major injuries should be dealt with by a vet, but if the wound is minor or bleeding, it can be useful to apply a dressing at home.

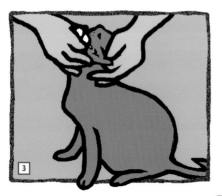

5. GETTING A CAT TO SWALLOW PILLS

Hold your cat's head so that you can open its mouth, then take the pill between the thumb and forefinger of your other hand, while using your middle finger to lower its jaw. Keep its head pointing upwards and quickly place the pill as far down its throat as possible. Close its jaw as soon as you have done this and keep its mouth closed, stroking its throat to encourage it to swallow. Unless the pill is placed right at the back of the throat, your cat will be able to spit it out. You can obtain a dosing gun from your vet if your cat is uncooperative.

6. GETTING A CAT TO SWALLOW LIQUID MEDICINES

Using the capsule of a syringe (without the needle!), insert it into the side of your cat's mouth. Keep its head up and slowly drip the liquid into its throat, then free the jaw. Medicines can also be hidden in food or drink.

7. GIVING EYE DROPS

Hold your cat from behind, tilt its head back, then push down the lower eyelid with your index finger. Use the other hand to squeeze the drops into the lower lid, without touching the eye. Do this from above the head so that the cat cannot see the applicator. Hold the eye shut for a moment so that the drops are distributed around the eye.

HYGIENE

Brushing

It is much easier to brush a cat that has become accustomed to being groomed when young. For the comfort of your cat, groom regularly and thoroughly. A short-haired cat needs to be brushed once a week with a soft brush, following the direction of the fur. A long-haired cat needs brushing daily with a metal comb and then with a brush.

Ears

Clean the ears with a cotton wool pad moistened with warm water or baby oil. Twist it gently inside the ears and then dry with a tissue.

Eyes

Weeping eyes should be cleaned up to twice a day using a separate cotton wool pad for each, wetted in an opthalmic solution.

Claws

Hold the cat's paw, pressing at the base of the claw so that it pops out of its hood, then trim the white tip, avoiding the pink quick, using special nail clippers.

Getting rid of fleas

Flea treatments vary in efficacy from impregnated collars and powders to the safe and highly-effective 'spot on' products now available from vets.

Preventing worms

Cats should be wormed during pregnancy, and kittens at four weeks. Indoor cats will then need a yearly dose. Outdoor cats should be treated every three months.

Emergency procedures

After a serious accident, your cat's life could be at risk. If you act quickly and appropriately, you could remove it from immediate danger and help to avoid complications. Here are a few tips to help you learn the right action to take in case of an emergency. Knowing how to give your animal first-aid could save its life!

1. BURNS

To soothe the pain, run some cold water over the burned area for several minutes. If it is a superficial burn, apply an oil-based ointment, but if it is a severe burn just cover it with a damp cloth and take your cat straight to the vet. For chemical burns, try to wash the substance off the cat immediately – unless the problem is minor, it is best to let your vet do this.

CAT DISEASES
See pages 112–115.

2. CUTS

Clean the wound with a pad that has been dampened with warm water, wiping from the centre of the wound outwards, then disinfect it with a mild antiseptic solution such as Savlon. If the skin is only grazed, you will need to apply some antiseptic powder or cream and a small dressing. If the wound is serious, or the underlying tissues have been affected, the cat will need stitches and you will have to take it to the vet within 24 hours.

3. HAEMORRHAGES

Spurts of bright red blood come from an artery; steady streams of darker blood come from a vein. Minor bleeding can usually be stopped by applying and maintaining pressure on a large gauze pad soaked in cold water. Bleeding should stop within a couple of minutes, but if it does not, secure the pad with a bandage and contact your vet. If an arterial haemorrhage occurs, you may need to apply a tourniquet made from a string, a tie or a belt. Contact a vet straight away. The tourniquet should stop the bleeding within a few seconds but, if left for longer than an hour, the tissues may start to turn gangrenous.

5. POISONING

The most common symptoms of poisoning are depression and weakness, salivation, vomiting and diarrhoea, sometimes accompanied by convulsions and walking difficulties. If poisoning is suspected, contact your vet immediately. If the coat is contaminated, wash or clip the substance away to avoid further ingestion. Only attempt to make your cat vomit (using a weak solution of salt-water) if it is impossible to get it to the vet's quickly. It is best to take your cat, and a sample of the toxic substance it has consumed, straight to a veterinary surgery.

4. FRACTURES

If your cat has fractured a limb, it will no longer be able to walk or lean on it because the area will be swollen and painful to touch. If it has fractured its spine, it will be paralysed from the break down. If your cat has cracked a rib, it may have difficulty breathing. A fracture to the skull will normally leave a cat unconscious. After falling from high up, it is quite common for a cat to fracture its hard palate, the bony part of the roof of the mouth. There will usually be bleeding from the nostrils and obvious signs of mouth pain. If your cat suffers a fracture, lie it in a large, secure box or basket and take it straight to the vet.

6. ABSCESSES

If bite wounds are not treated rapidly, they often become septic and abscesses may start to form, making the area swollen and tender. Clip the surrounding fur and try to bring the abscess to a head with frequent bathing and a hand-hot compress. If the abscess is large or does not burst within 24 hours, it may need to be lanced by a vet. Antibiotics may also be required to control the infection.

EMERGENCY CONTACT

If you cannot get to a veterinary surgery, contact a vet, who will have access to the Veterinary Poisions Information Service.

Dangers in the home

Because houses are designed for human beings, they can be dangerous places for unsuspecting animals. Try to be careful and vigilant, because accidents can easily happen.

If you leave a pan on the stove, make sure the handle is turned inwards.

Store your household products and any other toxic products out of your cat's reach. Keep your valuables safe too, even if they are not a danger to your cat!

Take care when doing repairs about the house. Cats love to explore new nooks and crannies, and a raised floorboard will prove irresistible. Make sure you know where your cat is before you seal floorboards etc. back down again.

Windows

If excited by the sight of a bird or fly, cats have been known to throw caution to the wind and try to take off after them! If you think there is a danger of this happening, it is a good idea to fit bars or nets across windows, balconies and terraces.

The kitchen

Cover hot-plates with a pan of cold water, and make sure your cat is not in the way when you are carrying a container of hot liquid. Keep cleaning products out of reach.

Plants

Many household plants can be poisonous, so make sure your cat does not have access to them. Certain types of grass can be provided to give your cat something to nibble on in the home.

Electrical equipment

Do not switch on the cooker, washing machine or the tumble dryer without first checking that your cat is not inside it – cats love to curl up in small places. Unplug the iron and leave it to cool out of your cat's reach. Hide all electrical cables behind furniture or under plastic covers, as burns and electrocution are not uncommon, especially with kittens.

Toxic products

Keep medication, anti-freeze and insecticides well out of your cat's reach. Do not close a cupboard or drawer without checking that the cat is not inside. Hide pins, needles and other sharp objects that could injure your cat, and place a guard in front of the fire. Young cats and kittens are particularly drawn to needles and threads.

Hide electric cables behind furniture because cats love to play with anything long and thin.

Be careful with rat poison and insecticides because they can have an effect on other animals too.

If you have an open fire, place a fireguard in front of it. Cats love to lounge by the fire and sometimes get too close.

Training and behavioural development

Kittens leave their mothers when they are about ten weeks old, having undergone the important stages in their behavioural development that condition their personalities and determine their capacity to adapt, mainly to humans. Training can, therefore, only reinforce the 'good manners' that they have learned and suppress any behaviour that bothers you.

Rules for mutual understanding

You need to be consistent and coherent if you want an animal to understand what you expect of it. Never accept behaviour that you would normally prohibit, because a cat will remember that it can break the rules. You will need to persevere with the rules you lay down, and it is essential that you keep calm – shouting makes cats nervous and less attentive. Always use the same words, preferably short ones, to tell it off. It is pointless scolding a cat any length of time after it has made a mistake because it will not be capable of making the link between the reprimand and the cause of your anger.

Scratching

Cats scratch to leave visible marks. Make scratchboards from materials such as carpet or rope, and stand them up around the house. If your cat starts scratching a piece of furniture, cover a scratchboard with a similar fabric and place it in front of the item. Encourage the use of the board; once in use, it can gradually be moved to a more convenient position. To dissuade your cat from scratching in a particular place, put some foil around it on the floor – the cat will be disturbed by the noise its paws make when it walks on it.

Aggressiveness

Aggressiveness can be genetic – aggressive parents will often have aggressive kittens. A stray cat, taken in when it is older than six weeks, may well have acquired an aggressive nature. In this case, you will have to allow it to develop at its own pace. Do not try to pick it up or stroke it, but speak often to it in a tender voice, and give it titbits from a distance. Aggressiveness caused by fear, anxiety or pain, is termed as 'reactional'.

Rewards

Stroking and words of praise are just as much rewards to your cat as games and titbits are. Any sort of reward will encourage your cat to behave well, so you should reward it whenever it is good.

Scolding

Imitation is a good way to tell your cat how you feel. When it is unhappy, it hisses and spits, so do the same. If it behaves badly, you can also blow into its face or, better still, squirt it with water from a plant sprayer. Do this without uttering a word, and avoid smacking it, as this will reinforce its bad behaviour.

Mess

Cats are creatures of habit, and the slightest changes in their environment can be enough to make them go to the toilet in inappropriate places. The arrival of a new pet is also a frequent cause of soiling. If your cat uses a litter tray, the litter must be regularly refreshed and deep enough for the cat to be able to scratch around in, as this act triggers bowel movement.

Protect your surroundings

We have little to fear from cats but, nonetheless, you should take certain hygiene precautions.

Transmissible diseases

Toxoplasmosis is one of the commonest parasitic diseases of animals and man. Cats are the only animal in which this organism can reproduce. The disease can cause abnormalities in the unborn children of pregnant women, and can be serious for people with weakened immune systems. It is transmitted in garden soil contaminated by cats and through poor hygiene when dealing with cat faeces. Fleas, ringworm, lice, mites, bacterial food poisoning and even tuberculosis can also sometimes be transmitted from cats to people.

Cat allergies

Unless you have consulted a specialist, avoid keeping a cat if someone in your house suffers from asthma, rashes or other allergies.

CATS AND CHILDREN

Teach children how to stroke a cat gently and how to recognise when it is irritated. Do not leave a very young child alone with a cat, and never let cats sleep in the same room as babies. Never let your children play near the cat's litter tray.

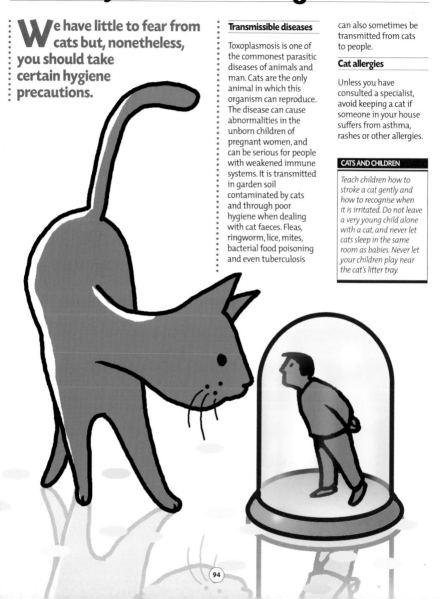

FIND OUT

FROM LOUIS WAIN TO FRITZ THE CAT, CATS HAVE PROVIDED THE MUSE FOR MANY AN ARTIST AND WRITER, THOUGH THEIR MIXED FORTUNES OVER THE YEARS HAVE NOT ALWAYS LED TO THEM BEING PORTRAYED IN THE MOST FAVOURABLE LIGHT. NEVERTHELESS, THEY HAVE BECOME VERY MUCH PART OF OUR SOCIETY. THIS CHAPTER WILL HELP YOU TO CHOOSE ONE THAT SUITS YOU AND LOOK AFTER IT RESPONSIBLY. USEFUL ADDRESSES TO FIND OUT MORE.

A place in the history of humankind

Despite their striking appearance and the beauty of their movements, cats featured very little in Western art before the beginning of the 19th century. On the other hand, cats have been worshipped in the art and literature of many Eastern cultures since ancient times.

Deified in ancient times

It is entirely thanks to the artists of Ancient Egypt that cats first entered the history of art. No other people depicted cats in their art to such an extent until the 19th century. Ancient Egyptians believed cats to be sacred, and many painters and sculptors linked the spirituality of cats to the gods, seeing them as a sign of life after death. Early depictions of cats were almost always religiously inspired, and therefore emphasised the animal's noble and saintly characteristics. Later, progressive vulgarisation of religious rites allowed artists to include more realism into their work and to draw inspiration from nature. This could, for example, give rise to a scene of a cat chasing and frightening birds in marshland, playing the role of a retriever. The Greeks and the Romans, who mocked the Egyptians for their veneration of cats, preferred to paint other members of the family, such as lions and tigers, whose majesty fitted in better with their gods' universe. Only a few bas-reliefs, vases and mosaics – notably one beautifully crafted piece discovered in Pompeii – reveal the discreet presence of cats in Greek and Roman society.

The Emperor of China's kittens

European bestiaries (books depicting both real and imaginary beasts) of the Middle Ages did not include cats, but they had already been widely represented in China. Because of the fragility of the materials used, the majority of ancient Oriental art has been lost. However, several painters of the Song dynasty (950–1279) reveal the importance of cats in Chinese high society in a very realistic style. One painting of this period, of kittens capering in a garden in spring, is attributed to the Emperor of China himself. In 13th-century Europe, cats were first featured in the sculptured masonry of various cathedrals, even though the Church still associated them with the devil. In Strasbourg, with reference to the *Fable of the Fox*, the cat Tibertius can be seen representing cunning and cruelty, handing the missal to the donkey-archpriest Bernard. A theme often taken up in illustrated animal books and in the 'hour books' that contained the daily prayers was that of the cat as a rat-catcher. Over the years, Western artists and writers gradually began to depict cats as family animals rather than always linking them with witchcraft or devilry. The cat's air of mystery, however, has meant that it has never quite managed to shake itself entirely free of such associations.

Cat sketches by
Lebrun.

Engraving by Jean-Baptiste Oudry, *Le vieux chat et la jeune souris* (The old cat and the young mouse).

Over the course of the following three centuries, the idea of the cat as a demonic being, slowly began to die out. Nonetheless, Cosimo Rosseli's *The Last Supper* in the Sistine Chapel (1481) uses a confrontation between a dog and a cat to illustrate the fight between good and evil, bearing witness to the continuing demonisation of cats. Dürer (1471–1528), painted a cat with a snake, associating it with the action that expelled Adam and Eve from Eden. In Tintoretto's *Supper* (1518–94), a cat appears at the feet of traitorous Judas. But people gradually started to speak out against this diabolic reputation of the poor cat. Artists like Pieter Brueghel the elder (1525–69) began to depict cats more favourably, denouncing the fate reserved for them by the likes of Hieronymous Bosch (1450–1516), who was certain that they had an evil nature.

In the 17th century, Le Nain, Callot, Jordaens and Velazquez depicted cats in the intimacy of rural homes and in scenes of daily life, representing their integration into domestic society. In the century that followed, Chardin (1699–1779) illustrated cats as greedy, thieving animals, but Watteau (1684–1721), Tiepolo (1696–1770) and then Fragonard (1732–1806) painted contented cats – in the arms of their mistresses or strutting about in luxurious aristocratic interiors.

Even in England, where cats were seen to embody all evil well into the 18th century, painters like William Hogarth (1697–1764) were beginning to include cats in their scenes of family life. Hogarth's painting of *The Graham Family*, includes a mischievous-looking tabby cat looking 'playfully' at a caged bird.

For various reasons, cats do not feature in paintings as often as dogs. They are solitary creatures that participate in our lives in a very independent way, whereas dogs follow people around, hunting with them and guarding their property. Even the shape of cats, which does not differ much from one breed to the next, does not offer painters as much choice as that of dogs, which can range from huge hounds to tiny lap dogs. Up until the Age of Enlightenment, cats were usually represented symbolically or were used simply as decoration in the paintings in which they featured – there are very few outstanding pictures of cats. We must mention however, among other minor masters, the French painter and naturalist Jean-Baptiste Oudry, who illustrated the renowned edition of *La Fontaine's Fables*, Fragonard's student Marguerite Gérard, for her *Petite fille jouant avec un chat emmailloté* and *Le Déjeuner du chat*, and also the painter of Hungarian origin Gottfried Mind (1768–1814) who, idolising cats, dedicated all his work in Berne to them, and was labelled the 'Raphael of cats' by his colleagues. These painters, however, hardly made a mark in the history of art. Their work, which could be termed as 'felineophilia', was later continued by artists such as the Dutch Henriette Ronner-Knip (1821–1909) and British cat caricaturist Louis Wain (1860–1939).

A source of inspiration for engravers

Meanwhile, in Japan, other artists were showing immense talent, making detailed observations of domestic cats, and presenting them in a range of styles.

Kitagawa Utamaro (1753–1806) soberly depicted serene scenes of family life in subtle tones. Hiroshige (1797–1858), the unrivalled master of engraving who was much admired by Monet, used only a few brush strokes to show the temptations and hesitations of a cat in front of a plate of shellfish. Utagawa Kuniyoshi (1797–1861) brought scenes to life in luxurious detail that would do justice to the best animal documentaries. His studio was always full of cats and his student, Kawanabe Gyosai (1831–89), left us a portrait of him grooming a cat as he held it in his arms. This is reminiscent of Tsuguharu Foujita's self-portraits (1886–1968). Foujita moved to Paris in 1913, and became friends with Picasso, often painting cats alongside women in scenes of an erotic nature.

The 19th-century passion for animals

In Europe, Romantic painting mirrored the literary trends of the end of the 19th century. The motivation behind these trends – the search for roots in the medieval past, communion with nature, and delvings into the subconscious – triggered the end of encyclopaedic rationalism. As Goya (1746–1828) wrote in 1797, 'The sleep of reason engenders monsters'.

In the collective subconscious, cats were still considered cunning, thieving, lazy and selfish. In his *Portrait of Don Manuel Osorio de Zuniga*, Goya shows three cats coveting a little boy's cake; much later, and in a completely different style, Walt Disney (1901–67) included two treacherous Siamese cats in *Lady and the Tramp*.

Even artists who claimed to like cats, such as Toulouse Lautrec and Mucha, represented

them with an evil glint in their eyes. French author Honoré de Balzac said of the cat, 'Heaven is in its eyes, hell is in its heart.' Of his own cat, Beauty, he wrote: 'She is the most sweet, clean, lithe, devoted and disloyal, attractive and dangerous animal.' Cats were perceived to have a kind of dual personality, and this caught the imagination of artists and writers alike. Oscar Wilde (1854–1900), T. S. Eliot (1888–1965), W. B. Yeats (1865–1939) and Edgar Allan Poe (1809–1849) all portrayed cats as beautiful and intelligent creatures, but with an underlying air of mystery and magic. Eliot's cunning, clever, aloof *Mr Mistofeles*, for example, is 'the original conjuring cat'. Pluto, the subject of Poe's horror tale *The Black Cat*, is described as a 'beautiful animal, entirely black, and sagacious to an astonishing degree', but he later goes on to exact a terrible revenge on his abusive owner.

Cats and love

Cats lead torrid love lives, and this characteristic became a source of inspiration for some artists. Given half a chance, cats will mate with a string of different partners in succession. This is actually a biological necessity, because female cats ovulate only after mating, and therefore need to mate several times in order to ensure conception. The composer Rossini was inspired by the endless moonlight serenades of cats – Champfleury identified 63 tones in a cat's vocal register – and put them to music in his *Duetto buffo dei due gatti*, much to the amusement of his female singers.

The unrestrained sensuality of both male and female cats has been used by Western painters to emphasise the same quality in their models, following the examples of the Japanese engravers, whose geishas were often depicted in the company of cats. This is why Edouard Manet (1832–1883) placed a black cat at the feet of his Olympia. In the painting, which he originally wanted to call 'Venus with a cat', he has substituted the small dog that appears in Titian's *Venus of Urbino*, which had inspired him, with a cat. Some critics were scandalised, writing that 'prudent young girls should shun this spectacle.' The Belgian Félicien Rops (1831–1898) almost always associated black cats with the frivolous women he depicted, as did many of the compositions inspired by the discovery of Ancient Egypt. Their painters lived in an Oriental fantasy world inhabited by naked women and cats. On the other hand, maybe in order to protect the modesty of his models, Auguste Renoir (1841–1919) painted them with cats draped languorously in their arms. Today, this artistic tradition is continued by painters such as Balthus, whose work has always featured cats. They help to create the erotic atmosphere that is central to his work. In a completely different realm, the authors of comic strips like Ralph Baskhi and Robert Crum with *Fritz the Cat* have exploited cats' lustful reputation in order to mock everything considered morally reproachable. Many films, such as Marcel Pagnol's *La femme du boulanger*, which was adapted from a novel by Jean Giono, have also used the lewdness that is attributed to female cats, to further stigmatise women.

The link between cats and negative attitudes towards women is age-old. The word 'moggie', now commonly used to describe a non-pedigree cat, was derived from a medieval term used to describe a loose woman or prostitute.

Nonetheless, it is perhaps, above all else, cats' grace, beauty and delicacy that make them such popular symbols of sensuality for artists and writers. Curvaceous, languorous, supple and elegant, the cat embodies many of the features considered most alluring in the female form.

Cats and mysticism

Cats regard us with an unwinking stillness, and it is hard for anybody being observed in such a way not to gaze back into their unfathomable eyes without attributing a certain wisdom and mysticism to their owner. This is another attribute of the cat that has inspired artists. In 1897, Paul Gauguin (1848–1903) painted the largest picture of his life, *D'où venons nous? Que sommes nous? Où allons nous?* (Where do we come from? Who are we? Where are we going?). There are two cats, the only two he ever painted, at the bottom of the picture beneath an imperious statue – one cat plays while the other sleeps, surrounded by figures of different ages, picking fruit, sleeping and in deep contemplation.

Tom and Jerry from the Hanna Barbera cartoon.

Cats in children's literature

Children's literature is full of feline characters, from Beatrix Potter's (1866–1943) mischievous Tom Kitten and the kindly Miss Moppet to T. S. Eliot's collection in *Old Possum's Book of Practical Cats*, written for adults and loved by children. Authors of children's books pick up on cats' playful natures, rather than any imagined darker side to their personalities. Potter's Miss Moppet, a tabby kitten with a pink bow around her neck, is the target of a dog's trick, reversing the cat's traditional role as a trickster. Tom Kitten is just as cute in his role as an inefficient mouse-catcher. Despite the little cat's efforts, the mouse is left dancing a jig on top of the cupboard at the end of the tale. The cats who populate T. S. Eliot's *Book of Practical Cats* take on a surprising range of personalities, from the mysterious Macavity who steals Admiralty charts and outwits Scotland Yard to the thespian Gus (short for Asparagus) who knew seventy speeches by heart and once understudied Dick Whittington's Cat.

Saved by a caricature

Many of the cats featured in childrens' literature have human characteristics – they speak, they wear clothes, and even eat pies and do magic tricks. It is certainly thanks to the caricature that cats have broken free from the stereotypical roles most often given to them by artists, of cunning, thieving, sexually obsessed, possessed creatures.

Louis Wain's paintings of anthropomorphic cats in amusing poses touched the hearts of the Victorian public. He began by sketching his own cat to cheer his sick wife up, and things took off from there. He painted cats sledging, cats carol singing, and even cats tucked up in bed. Thousands of children grew up with his playful, humorous, human-like cats decorating their nursery walls. He presented cats in a totally accessible way, not as mysterious creatures, but as small, furry versions of people. This was important in bringing about the acceptance of the cat as part of the family rather than as a shadowy presence lurking on the edge of our world.

FABLES AND NURSERY RHYMES

The earliest literary descriptions of cats, found in Greek and Latin fables, are of wicked and untrustworthy animals. Aesop and Phaedrus, in particular, fixed certain ideas about the nature of cats in the collective subconscious. These preconceptions were later reiterated by French author La Fontaine (1621–1695) in his version of these ancient animal tales:

'The cat and the fox,
like beautiful little saints
 Went on a pilgrimage.
They were both hypocrites,
two wheedlers.'

Everybody remembers stories like *Puss in Boots*, by Charles Perrault (1628–1703), in which the cat is loyal yet cunning and ambitious. Texts like these have spread an unflattering image of the cat, strengthened, further by popular nursery rhymes, such as:

'Six little mice sat down to spin;
Pussy passed by and she peeped in ...
Shall I come in and cut off your threads?
No, no, Mistress Pussy, you'd bite
off our heads ...
Your house is the nicest I see,
I think there is room for you and for me.
The mice were so pleased that they
opened the door,
And Pussy soon had them all dead
on the floor.'

Cartoon cats

With the increasing popularity of cartoons and animated films, the 20th century marked a new era in the artistic representation of cats. The feline form lent itself well to these mediums, and the list of cat stars is almost endless – from *Top Cat* to *Garfield*, *Tom and Jerry* to *The Aristocats*, *Henry's Cat* to *The Cat in the Hat*. In keeping with tradition, these cartoon cats are often crafty – Tom incessantly chases Jerry and The Cat in the Hat and Henry's Cat spend all their time hatching devious plots, but above all they are loveable and amusing. The cartoonists have chosen to emphasise these aspects of feline nature, and, to the younger generation at least, cats may finally have lost their bad reputation.

Film stars

Cats have not fared quite so favourably in film. The infamous Bond villain Blofeld, whose face wasn't even shown in his early films, was always depicted stroking a white persian cat. This began a craze for copycats, mimicked first of all by the villain in *Inspector Gadget* and later in the *Austin Powers* films. Dr Evil, the spoof villain in *Austin Powers*, is constantly fawning over a white persian cat called Mr Bigglesworth. Used in this way, almost like witches familiars, the cat becomes symbolic of the sinister. It is also somehow ingenuous that the beautiful cat is being lovingly petted by a villain plotting to take over the world to his own evil advantage.

Which artists have tried to depict cats just as they are, regardless of the fantasies they evoke? The list is long – Géricault, Delacroix, Courbet, Marquet, Valadon, Vollard, Klee, Dufy, Giacometti, Miró, Andy Warhol, etc. One name that stands out among all these is that of Swiss artist Théophile Alexandre Steinlein (1859–1923). He was the creator of the famous poster – Le Chat Noir – which advertised the Montmartre cabaret show that the whole of literary and artistic Paris flocked to at the end of the 19th century. Steinlein was nicknamed 'the man of a hundred thousand cats' because he kept so many at his house in Montmartre. Another important name in this genre is a Bavarian called Franz Marc (1880–1916), whose statuesque depictions show what a cat's rapid movements hide. The style of Pierre Bonnard (1867–47) is equally significant because his paintings show cats just as we experience them in everyday life. Last but by no means least is Pablo Picasso (1881–1973). In works like *The Bath* (1905), where a cat is shown watching a family bathing, the animal is very much part of family life. *Cat and Bird* (1939) shows the wilder side of the cat, with sharp claws and prey gripped between its teeth. Picasso thus reminds us of the cat's dual personality – the pet that is capable of mutating into a wild animal as soon as the front door is opened: 'I want to create a cat like the ones I see on the road. They have nothing in common with pet cats, their coat is ruffled and they run like devils.' At the turn of the century, cats were finally freed of the prejudices that had affected them for so long.

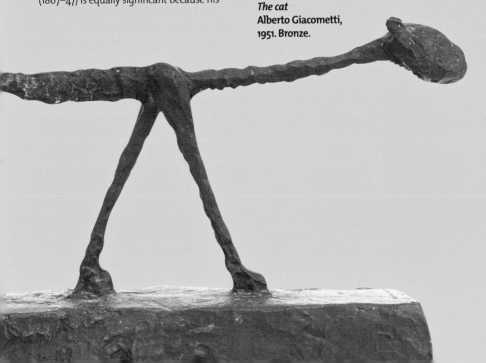

The cat
Alberto Giacometti,
1951. Bronze.

The cat as a muse for writers and poets

Cats have a reputation for being the work companions of writers and poets. Their beauty, and the mysterious link that binds them to human beings, have inspired many beautiful, amusing and enduring works of literature.

The Owl and the Pussy-cat

The Owl and the Pussy-cat went to sea
  In a beautiful pea green boat,
They took some honey, and plenty of money,
  Wrapped up in a five pound note.
The Owl looked up to the stars above,
  And sang to a small guitar,
'O lovely Pussy! O Pussy my love
  What a beautiful Pussy you are,
    You are,
    You are!
What a beautiful Pussy you are!'

Pussy said to the Owl, 'You elegant fowl!
  How charmingly sweet you sing!
O let us be married! too long we have tarried:
  But what shall we do for a ring?'
They sailed away, for a year and a day,
  To the land where the Bong-tree grows
And there in a wood a Piggy-wig stood
  With a ring at the end of his nose,
    His nose,
    His nose,
With a ring at the end of his nose.

Dear pig, are you willing to sell for one
  shilling
Your ring?' Said the Piggy, 'I will.'

So they took it away, and were married next
  day
  By the Turkey who lives on the hill.
They dined on mince, and slices of quince,
  Which they ate with a runcible spoon;
And hand in hand, on the edge of the sand,
  They danced by the light of the moon,
    The moon,
    The moon,
They danced by the light of the moon.

Edward Lear The Owl and the Pussy-cat

The Sphinx

… This curious cat
Lies crouching on the Chinese mat with
eyes of satin rimmed with gold.
Upon the mat she lies and leers
and on the tawny throat of her
Flutters the soft and fur
or ripples to her pointed ears.
Come forth my lovely seneschal!
So somnolent, so statuesque! …
Let me touch those curving claws
of yellow ivory and grasp
The tail that like a monstrous Asp coils
round your heavy velvet paws!

Oscar Wilde The Sphinx, *extract*

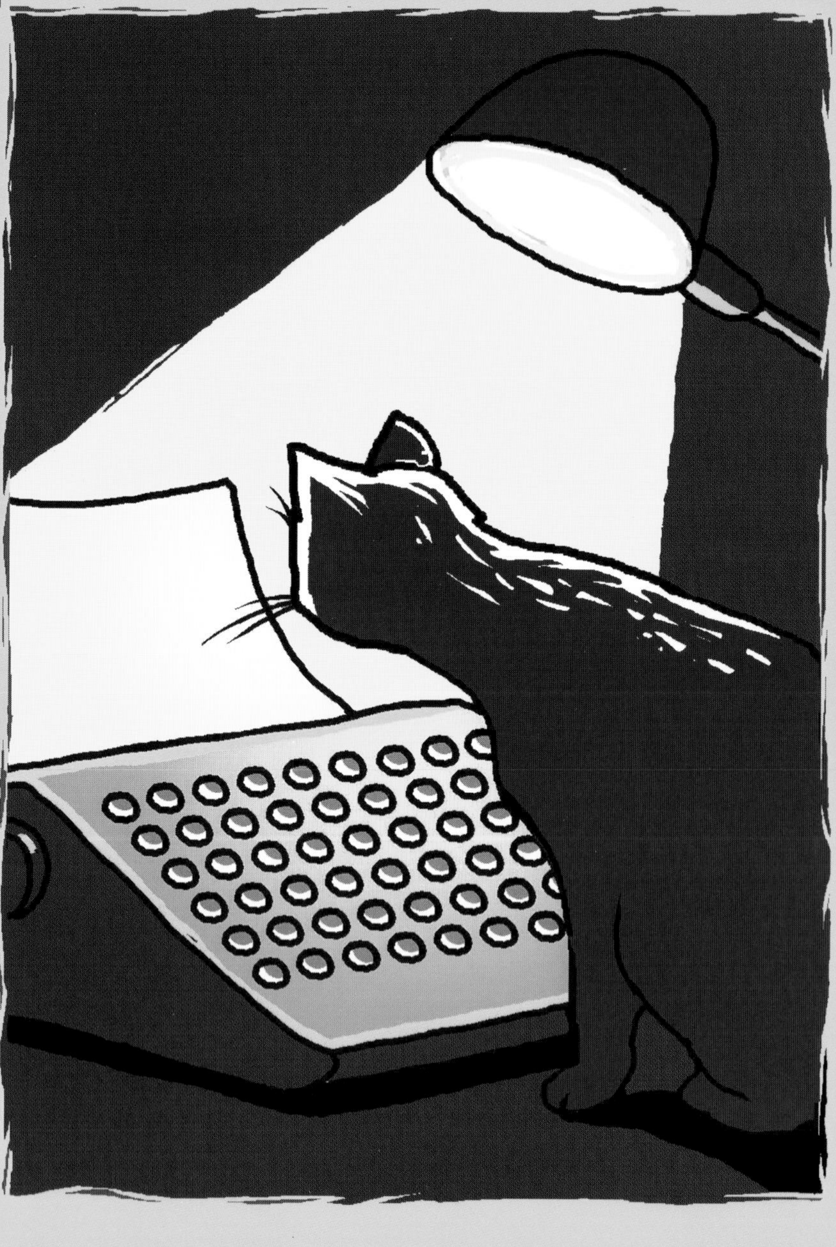

Alice's Adventures in Wonderland
Lewis Carroll (1832–1898)

The Cheshire Cat only grinned when it saw Alice. It looked good-natured, she thought: still it had *very* long claws and a great many teeth, so she felt that it ought to be treated with respect. 'Cheshire Puss,' she began, rather timidly, as she did not know at all whether it would like the name: however, it only grinned a little wider. 'Come, it's pleased so far,' thought Alice, and she went on. 'Would you tell me, please, which way I ought to go from here?'

'That depends a good deal on where you want to get to,' said the Cat.

'I don't much care where –' said Alice.

'Then it doesn't matter which way you go,' said the Cat.

'– so long as I get *somewhere*,' Alice added as an explanation.

'Oh, you're sure to do that,' said the Cat, 'if you only walk long enough.'

Alice felt that this could not be denied, so she tried another question. 'What sort of people live about here?'

'In that direction,' said the Cat, waving its right paw round, 'lives a Hatter: and in *that* direction,' waving the other paw, 'lives a March Hare. Visit either you like: they're both mad.'

'But I don't want to go among mad people,' Alice remarked.

'Oh, you can't help that,' said the Cat: 'we're all mad here. I'm mad. You're mad.'

'How do you know I'm mad?' said Alice.

'You must be,' said the Cat, 'or you wouldn't have come here.'

Alice didn't think that proved it at all; however, she went on 'And how do you know that you're mad?'

'To begin with,' said the Cat, 'a dog's not mad. You grant that?'

'I suppose so,' said Alice.

'Well then,' the Cat went on, 'you see a dog growls when it's angry, and wags its tail when it's pleased. Now I growl when I'm pleased and wag my tail when I'm angry. Therefore, I'm mad.'

'I call it purring not growling,' said Alice.

'Call it what you like,' said the Cat. 'Do you play croquet with the Queen today?'

'I should like it very much,' said Alice, 'but I haven't been invited yet.'

'You'll see me there,' said the Cat, and vanished.

Alice was not much surprised at this, she was getting so used to queer things happening. While she was looking at the place where it had been, it suddenly appeared again ...

... 'I wish you wouldn't keep appearing and vanishing so suddenly: you make one quite giddy.'

'All right,' said the Cat; and this time it vanished quite slowly, beginning with the end of the tail, and ending with the grin, which remained some time after the rest if it had gone.

'Well, I've often seen a cat without a grin,' thought Alice, 'but a grin without a cat! It's the most curious thing I ever saw in all my life!'

The legal world of cats

Fortunately, there are laws to protect domestic animals. Under the Protection of Animals Act 1911, it is an offence to treat a cat or kitten cruelly; cause unnecessary suffering; poison a cat or kitten; or carry out an operation without 'due care and humanity'. Prosecution can result from carrying out any of these offences, and also from allowing them to take place. If an act of cruelty results in injury or damage to a cat, the perpetrator can be prosecuted under the Criminal Damage Act 1971. Unlicenced painful experiments are usually considered an offence under the Cruelty to Animals Act 1876.

A cat's 'identity card'

Cat owners in the UK are not obliged to have their pets microchipped or tatooed, unless they are travelling abroad with them. But it is worth getting identification for your cat, in case it goes missing. Microchipping involves the insertion of a tiny electronic transponder under the skin on the neck. When swiped with a handheld scanner, the chip emits a unique code, which is held in a central database. Vets and rescue organisations use scanners to reunite lost pets with their owners.

Things that a cat must have for travel

To travel abroad under the Pets Travel Scheme (PETS), your cat must be identified with an appropriate microchip and vaccinated successfully against rabies. You must obtain a PETS certificate from a government-approved vet. Your cat must be treated against ticks and tapeworm just before its return to this country through certain designated ports.

Aspects of travel

When animals are accompanied by their owners on a private journey, or if the transport is not of a commercial nature, the Welfare of Animals (Transport) Act 1997 covers them. The Act states that 'No person shall transport any animal in a way that causes or is likely to cause injury or unnecessary suffering to that animal.' Commercial carriers are placed under certain further obligations by other provisions of the Order. Be aware that laws regarding cats vary from country to country. It is illegal to bring a cat or kitten into the UK by private boat or plane.

Obligations of owners

In most cases, if you keep more than 12 cats in your home, the Local Authority may consider that you are actually running a cat sanctuary, something that requires planning permission. Because cats and kittens are not generally considered as 'livestock' under the Animal

Act 1971, your cat cannot commit trespass, and you cannot be held responsible for any damage it causes. Similarly, cats are not covered by the Road Traffic Act. However, consistent fouling of neighbours' gardens by your cat may be considered a health hazard under the Environmental Protection Act 1990: this measure also provides for complaints regarding 'nuisance' caused by animals.

Buying a cat or kitten

Because of their curious legal position, a cat or kitten is unlikely to be covered by the Sale of Goods Act. A clear written contract, containing all relevant details and conditions may be advisable. Get your new pet checked by your vet as soon as possible if there is any concern. If a problem is apparent, some redress may be available from the breeder if this has been agreed previously. A cat or kitten bought from a breeder of pedigree animals is usually accompanied by a document (pedigree) showing the cat's family going back three or more generations. It should also come with a breed number, registration number and the name and address of the breeder; details of vaccinations (including certificate) and worming, and information concerning the diet of your cat or kitten. If you have bought your pedigree cat solely as a pet, you may be required to have it neutered at an early age.

> **If you have lost or found a cat:**
>
> If you are registered, call the pet register. Otherwise, contact local and national pet rescue organisations, local veterinary surgeries and local radio stations.
>
> You could also try putting up 'lost' or 'missing' notices in local shops.

Cats and diseases

Cats often try to conceal their suffering, but some signs of illness or pain are clear. The cat will hide away, greet you with less affection than usual, and will not seek out caresses. It may also sleep more, go off its food or become irritable.

Clear signs

Some signs are a particularly strong indication that something is wrong – the appearance of a third eyelid partially covering the eye (this transparent membrane is normally concealed inside the eye); lying in the sphinx position, with the head between the paws; lack of elasticity of the skin, which takes longer to settle back into place if you pinch it.

Serious symptoms

Certain other symptoms could be the first signs of a serious illness, and you should contact your vet immediately if your cat displays them:

It sneezes and has a runny nose: in weaker cats (those that are very old or young or that have a weakened response to infection), these apparently minor symptoms could be the first signs of a more serious respiratory disease.
Unwillingness to exercise and coughing when exercising or laboured breathing.
It has persistent vomiting and/or diarrhoea, particularly if blood is present.
It is persistently constipated.
It has markedly increased thirst.
It has trouble passing urine or unusually frequent attempts are made (especially in unusual places), or the presence of blood in the urine.
It shows signs of uncoordination, paralysis, twitching, seizures, or is generally behaving very strangely.

At the vet's

To take your cat to the vet, you need a basket, box or bag that opens at the top, so that the surgeon can take the cat out by the scruff of the neck without being bitten or scratched. Avoid sitting next to a noisy dog in the waiting room and talk to your pet to reassure it. During the visit, keep calm and quietly describe the abnormal symptoms to the vet. He or she may ask you to leave the cat alone with them, as animals are often very receptive to their owner's stress.

An older cat's health

Signs of old age in cats are often subtle. However, many cats become old quite suddenly (over the course of a year or so) after the age of ten. Older cats become less active and sleep more; they often pay less attention to their coats, which become duller. Their teeth become prone to accumulating tartar, and sometimes rot and fall out. Outdoor territories become smaller. Old cats often become very set in their ways, and in some cases their personality may change. Some cats become less good-natured due to certain symptoms of old age, including an overactive thyroid, discomfort from arthritis or bad teeth, or liver or kidney disease. Other elderly cats suffer from 'senility' and, when they are not sleeping, revert to demanding, kitten-like behaviour.

The sad event

Unfortunately, a cat's life span is about five times shorter than ours, so it invariably leaves us 'too soon'. Some cats pass away peacefully at home, but others start to suffer near the end. If your cat is very unwell and its pain and distress cannot be relieved, it might be kinder to have it put to sleep.

If you have a garden, you may choose to bury it there by digging a deep hole, a good distance away from any buildings, wells or rivers. The other option is cremation. If you opt for collective cremation, it will cost you approximately £25. An individual cremation will cost about £70, but you can take the ashes away in a small urn. Pet cemeteries are rare and expensive. Your vet should be able to help you to arrange the disposal of your deceased pet.

Serious infectious diseases in cats

A cat's nine lives are of no use when it comes to avoiding serious viral infections. Vaccinations are an effective means of prevention in many cases, but unfortunately there is not a vaccine for every disease.

Cat flu

This disease is caused by feline calici virus (FCV) or feline herpes virus (FHV). The virus is present in the saliva, tears and nasal secretions of infected cats (FCV is also shed in the faeces). The main method of spread is by direct contact. The disease starts with sneezing, which gradually becomes worse. The eyes and nose weep and run. The cat will seem exhausted and its appetite will suffer. Its coat becomes dull, and its temperature may reach 40°C. Most cats will recover within a week or two, but in young kittens and cats with a weak immune system pneumonia may result. Recovered cats may carry FHV for life, and may suffer repeated bouts of flu. The vet should be contacted within a few days of the first symptoms appearing.

Feline infectious enteritis (Feline parvovirus)

This disease has been almost eliminated by vaccination, but can still cause problems in rescue centres and pet shops, and for breeders. Susceptible animals usually pick up the virus from a contaminated environment. Unvaccinated kittens are most at risk, after the protection conferred by their mothers has waned at about four to 12 weeks. Unvaccinated adults can also be infected. Signs of infection include vomiting and profuse, sometimes bloody, diarrhoea. Affected animals will be depressed and dehydrated and may sit hunched over their bowls without eating or drinking. Kittens of infected mothers may be born with impaired coordination. Early treatment is vital, and will consist of symptomatic and supportive measures.

CALENDAR OF VACCINATIONS – THESE MAY VARY ACCORDING TO MANUFACTURER'S INSTRUCTIONS, ASK YOUR VET FOR ADVICE.			
DISEASE	**1ST VACCINATION**	**2ND VACCINATION**	**BOOSTERS**
Parvovirus	9 weeks old	3 to 4 weeks later	Every other year
Cat 'flu	9 weeks old	3 to 4 weeks later	Every year
Feline Leukaemia	9 weeks old	3 to 4 weeks or 15 to 21 days later	Every year
Rabies	4 or 11 weeks old	12 weeks old or 2 to 4 weeks after 1st dose	Every year or every other year

Feline leukaemia virus (FeLV)

Feline leukaemia virus leads to deficiency of the immune system. It is present in the saliva of infected cats and is mainly transmitted by close contact. Kittens under four months of age are thought to be particularly at risk from permanent infection, as are unvaccinated adults entering environments where the infection is prevalent. Many cats will recover, but for cats that become permanently infected the outlook is bad. Symptoms may develop months or years after infection, and can be vague. Cats that seem listless or are susceptible to infections, and females that have unhealthy litters of kittens may be infected. FeLV can also result in cancers, most commonly affecting the glands, the bowel, the kidneys or the nervous system. Paired blood tests (carried out 12 to 16 weeks apart) will screen for the infection. It is also wise to carry out blood tests when a new animal comes into a house where there are already cats. There are vaccines available against FeLV.

Feline immunodeficiency virus (FIV)

Another virus that impairs the body's response to infection, FIV is thought to be spread mainly by bites and is most common in feral and free-roaming cats. Once the infection takes hold, the cat is permanently infected. Symptoms are varied, and are usually related to other diseases, which the cat becomes less able to fight. They include inflammation of the gums, diarrhoea and skin and respiratory infections. Cats may also suffer from kidney failure and central nervous system problems. Blood tests screen for the disease, but there is no vaccine. Treatment is aimed at the secondary infections. Whether or not to allow infected cats access to the outside world is a question of ethics.

Feline infectious peritonitis (FIP)

Caused by the feline corona virus (FCoV), 90 per cent of infected cats do not develop FIP. The disease is transmitted in the saliva and faeces of infected cats. Especially at the beginning, the symptoms of this disease are not very obvious. The cat will be tired, dejected, will lose its appetite, have digestive and respiratory disorders and run a temperature. The disease can then evolve in one of two different phases: the exudative (abnormal accumulation of liquid in the chest or abdomen) or the dry form (localised inflammation of several organs). There is no effective treatment, nor is there yet a vaccine available in the UK against this fatal disease. For the same reasons as with FeLV and FIV, a screening test is advisable.

Rabies

Methods of rabies prevention can be very effective, as is shown by the fact that, here in Britain, the disease has been almost entirely eradicated. The incidence of rabies has fallen dramatically throughout western Europe over the last ten years, but it is still a problem in eastern Europe and in Turkey, where pets can contract the disease from wild animals through biting, scratching and licking.

Small but determined

Cats have been through a lot of ups and downs over the centuries. Nowadays, they are often pampered, but in the past they have been both adored and martyrised. They have also been known to make themselves useful. Here are a few anecdotes.

Heroic cats and astonishing feats

One night in 1416, English soldiers seized the town of Meaux in north-eastern France. A barber called Etienne Terfaut was standing guard on the ramparts. When he saw the shadows of enemies prowling nearby, he decided to confuse them and amuse himself. He shaped his fur hat in such a fashion as to resemble the silhouette of a cat, and began to meow. However, a passing patrol caught him and locked him up in the dungeon for deserting his post. Convinced that his end was drawing near, the barber waited in fear for his sentence. But suddenly he was told that he had been appointed sergeant! His trick had worked so well that the English had withdrawn. His clowning had convinced them that the French were still strong enough to resist as they had not yet been forced to eat cats.

A cat's sense of direction, enabling it to find its way back home, sometimes over incredible distances, is another source of wonder to us, and another source of anecdotes. The 1600s were hard times for cats but, despite this, one pet cat accomplished an amazing feat. In 1601, the Earl of Southampton was imprisoned in the Tower of London by Queen Elizabeth I for his part in a rebellion against her. The earl's black and white cat, left alone in the earls' London home, missed his owner and set out to find him. All alone, the little cat found his way across the city to the Tower of London, where he prowled the roofs and battlements until he sensed his master was near. Having located

the earl's chamber, the faithful pet slipped down the chimney into the arms of his condemned owner. A painting has survived to this day of the earl with his cat beside him. A more recent example is this story of a New York vet and his pet cat. The vet moved to California, leaving his cat with his neighbours. Several months later, an emaciated cat entered his surgery and curled up in his armchair for a nap, as if he were part of the family. The cat looked remarkably like his old one, but the vet wanted to make sure. He remembered that his cat had a bone malformation in its tail. He examined the stray and found that he was the same cat! The stubborn moggie had beaten the record for distance covered on all fours – including detours – estimated at more than 7,000 kilometres (4,350 miles).

Other cats have also made it into the book of records, sometimes against their will. One cat fell from the 32nd floor of a block of flats, and came out unscathed! Imagine his fear when, 25 metres (82 feet) from the ground, he had already reached a speed of 90 kilometres (35 miles) per hour.

The record for the largest litter is held by an American cat who gave birth to 13 kittens. The size and weight record is held by Himmy, a tabby cat from Queensland, Australia, which died in 1986. He was 97 centimetres (38 inches) long, excluding his tail, and weighed 21 kilograms (46 pounds). He measured 84 centimetres (33 inches) around the middle.

A cat for everyone

There are character similarities between cats and humans. If you are looking for a cat to share your life, read on. Choose the seven character traits that seem to describe your personality best from the list below. Add up all the (A)s, (B)s, (C)s, (D)s and (E)s to find out which kind of cat suits you best.

❑ You like to be surprised. **C**

❑ You like tranquillity and soft cushions. **A**

❑ You prefer one-to-one contact to noisy get-togethers. **A**

❑ You do not get on with quiet or reserved people. **B**

❑ You like to spring surprises on people and appreciate unusual things. **D**

❑ You appreciate a strong character that is tempered by sensitivity. **A**

❑ You have a good sense of humour. **D**

❑ You like soft curves. **E**

❑ You are a good listener and patient. **B**

❑ You respect other people's independence. **B**

❑ Life for you is one long cuddle. **E**

❑ You do not mind if people are always following you around. **B**

❑ You are not upset by moodiness or sulking if it precedes moments of great tenderness. **A**

❑ You appreciate compact shapes and spectacular beauty. **A**

❑ You like trees. **C**

❑ You do not think that curiosity is a fault. **B**

❑ You still like to play with dolls. **E**

❑ You understand mood swings between affection and indifference. **C**

❑ You like a strong personality. **B**

❑ You don't object to people who express their feelings vehemently and have original tastes. **D**

❑ You need serenity in your life. **E**

❑ You are reassuring and know how to help to ease over-sensitivity. **B**

❑ You are attracted by simple shapes. **B**

ANSWERS:

– Mainly (A)s: You would get on well with a Persian.

– Mainly (B)s: You are the ideal companion for a Siamese, and are also suitable for Oriental cats in general, but to a lesser extent.

– Mainly (C)s: The European Cat and its cousins the British and American Shorthairs, the French Chartreux and the British Blue would all be happy with you.

– Mainly (D)s: You will have plenty of fun with the Sphinx (a cat that hardly has any hair at all), the Scottish Fold (with flat ears that form a kind of cap), or the American Curl (whose ears seem to join at the top of its head).

– Mainly (E)s: You would like the sweet Sacred Cat of Burma (which has white 'gloves') or the cool Ragdoll (the most relaxed cat of all).

Cats and proverbs

Cats have provided inspiration for many proverbs from all over the world. Some are easy to understand, others less so. For each proverb there is a corresponding meaning. Some are quite obvious, but others are more obscure. Have fun matching them up.

The proverbs

1) A clever kitten can turn around even in a little space. (French)

2) Nobody wants to put the bell around a cat's neck. (French)

3) Never buy a cat in a bag. (Danish)

4) Cats are tigers to rats. (Indian)

5) Covered milk will not be drunk by cats. (Bulgarian)

6) That will happen when cats grow horns and the Dutch get circumcised. (Malay)

7) A cat that becomes a monk does not forget its habits. (Ethiopian)

8) As soon as you treat it as a wild cat, it will start stealing chickens. (Madagascan)

9) Cats love to eat fish but hate to get their paws wet. (Ancient Latin)

The meaning

I) It is better to ask to see the merchandise before you pay for it.

H) A good workman never blames his tools.

F) There is always someone stronger than you.

E) It is better not to be the first to face danger.

A) A habit does not make a monk.

D) He or she enjoys the benefits without putting in any of the effort.

G) You have nothing to fear if you take the necessary precautions.

B) Pigs might fly (it will never happen).

C) An unjustified bad reputation leads to bad behaviour.

ANSWERS

1H - 2E - 3I - 4F - 5G - 6B - 7A - 8C - 9D

Cats and preconceptions

There are all sorts of rumours about cats. Are they true or false?

1. Cats purr because they are happy.

True   False

2. A well-fed cat will not hunt.

True   False

3. It is a world-wide superstition that black cats bring bad luck.

True   False

4. House cats do not need to be vaccinated.

True   False

5. Cat hairs cause allergies.

True   False

6. Cats grow fond of places, not of people.

True   False

7. Cats are perfectly happy to be alone.

True   False

ANSWERS

1. False. Cats also purr when sick or worried.
2. False. Hunting is instinctive for cats. If they are not hungry they do not eat their prey.
3. False. In the UK, if a black cat crosses your path it will bring you luck.
4. False. Some contagious diseases can be transmitted by insects (flies, mosquitoes) and by the owner if he or she has been in contact with an infected animal.
5. False. It is not the fur that causes allergies, it is a protein contained in its saliva, which the cat leaves on its fur when it cleans itself.
6. False. It is just as attached to its owner as it is to its house. However, cats are creatures of habit and they do not like moving house.
7. True. If this means that a cat is always capable of hunting in order to get food.
False, if this means that it does not need attention. If left alone, a cat can fall ill and even die.

For further information

▼

FELINE ORGANISATIONS

FELINE ADVISORY BUREAU
Taeselbury
High Street
Tisbury
Wiltshire SP3 6LD
Tel: 01747 871872
Website: www.fabcats.org
E-mail: fab@fabcats.org

THE GOVERNING COUNCIL OF CAT FANCY
4-6 Penel Orlieu
Bridgwater
Somerset TA6 3PG
Tel: 01278 427 575

INTERNATIONAL FELINE FEDERATION
Little Dene
Lenham Heath
Maidstone
Kent ME17 2BS
Tel: 01622 850913

PROTECTION SOCIETIES

CATS PROTECTION
17 Kings Road
Horsham
West Sussex RH13 5PN
Tel: 01403 221900
Website: www.cats.org.uk
E-mail: cpl@cats.org

RSPCA (ROYAL SOCIETY FOR THE PREVENTION OF CRUELTY TO ANIMALS)
Causeway, Horsham
West Sussex RH12 1HG
Tel: 0870 5555999
(emergencies only)
Website: www.rspca.org.uk
The oldest animal cruelty prevention organisation in the world, and older than the British police force. Its work is supported by a team of inspectors and an extensive volunteer network.

THE WOODGREEN ANIMAL SHELTER
King's Bush Farm
London Road
Godmanchester
Cambridgeshire
PE29 2NH
Tel: 01480 830014

THE BLUE CROSS ANIMAL WELFARE ASSOCIATION
Home Close Farm
Shilton Road
Burford
Oxon OX18 4PF
Tel: 01993 822651
Website:
www.thebluecross.org.uk
E-mail:
info@bluecross.org.uk
The Blue Cross is a hundred-year-old organisation that looks after unwanted and abandoned animals, and finds new homes for them when it can. It also produces a series of animal welfare leaflets.

LOTHIAN CAT RESCUE
Brewers Bush
Cockpen Road
Bonnyrigg
Midlothian
Scotland
Tel: 01875 821025

LANCASHIRE PET RESCUE
33 New Lane
Penwortham
Preston PR19JH
Tel: 01772 750263

PORTSMOUTH AND DISTRICT CAT RESCUE
94 Emsworth Road
North End
Portsmouth
Hampshire
Tel: 02392 646143

CLYDE VALLEY CAT RESCUE
Mousemill
Mousemill Road
Lanark ML11 9UG
Tel: 01698 881453

SHIRRIN RESCUE FOR PERSIAN CATS
Mallams
Broad Oak
Sturminster Newton
Dorset DT10 2HD
Tel: 01258 472073
E-mail: shirrin@aol.com

HOLLY HEDGE SANCTUARY
Wild Country Lane
Barrow Gurney
Bristol BS48 3SE
Tel: 01275 474719

SOCIETIES AND OTHER ORGANISATIONS

THE ASSOCIATION OF PET BEHAVIOUR COUNSELLORS
PO Box 46
Worcester WR8 9YS
Tel: 01386 751151

BRITISH VETERINARY ASSOCIATION
7 Mansfield Street
London W1G 9NQ
Tel: 020 7637 4769
Website: www.bva.co.uk
E-mail: bvahq@bva.co.uk

Internet

▼

SOME USEFUL WEBSITES

PET VET
www.petvet.demon.co.uk
This small animal site has advice on healthcare, feeding and bereavement, with useful links to other related pages.

PEDIGREE CATS
www.pedigreecat.co.uk
Photos and information about pedigree cats available in the UK, with links to breeders and registers.

CAT FANCIERS ASSOCIATION
www.fanciers.com
Site compiled by vets, breeders, show judges and exhibitors, with information on breeds, veterinary care, shows and clubs. Also check out the online bookstore.

AND ALSO ...
Some amusing sites:

www.thecatbasket.
freeserve.co.uk

www.cat-chat.co.uk

www.moggies.co.uk

www.pets-pyjamas.co.uk

Practical services

CATTERIES

COSY CATS CATTERY
Sinton Green Lane
Grimley
Near Worcester
WR2 6LP
Tel: 01905 641587

ELITE CATTERY
512 Archway Road
Highgate
London N6 4NA
Tel: 020 8340 5120

CEMETERIES AND CREMATORIA

PET CREMATORIUM AND CEMETERY
Wigan Road
Leyland
Preston
Lancashire BB8 0AA
Tel: 01772 622466

THE ORCHARD PET CEMETERY
Bohemia
The Old Kennels
Eridge Park
Tunbridge Wells
Kent TN3 9HA
Tel: 01892 750936

THE PET CREMATORIUM LTD
Baird Avenue
Strutherhill Industrial Estate
Larkhall
Lanarkshire ML9 2PJ
Tel: 01698 888500

COMMUNITY CLINICS

PDSA (PEOPLES' DISPENSARY FOR SICK ANIMALS)
Whitechapel Way
Priorslee
Telford
Shropshire TF2 9PQ
Tel: 01952 290999

EMERGENCY SERVICES

VETERINARY POISONS INFORMATION CENTRE
Tel: 020 7635 9195 or
0113 143 0715

THE VETERINARY EMERGENCY TREATMENT SERVICE
180 Merthyr Road
Whitchurch
Cardiff
Tel: 029 2052 9446
Some local newspapers print the details of the emergency veterinary surgeon who is on duty.

INSURANCE

PET PLAN LTD
Computer House
Great West Road
Brentford
Middlesex TW8 9DX
Tel: 0800 072 7000

PINNACLE PET HEALTHCARE PLC
New Horizons
Studio Way
Borehamwood
Hertfordshire WD6 5XX
Tel: 0845 2000738

LOST CATS

PET SEARCH UK
Tel: 01225 705175

DETECT-A-PET
Tel: 01628 525485

CATS PROTECTION LEAGUE LOST AND FOUND SERVICE
Tel: 01403 221900

TRAVEL ADVICE

THE PETS HELPLINE
Tel: 0870 241 1710

Cat magazines

CAT WORLD
Avalon Court
Star Road
Partridge Green
West Sussex RH13 8RY
Tel: 01403 711511

YOUR CAT MAGAZINE
FREEPOST
LE5981
Leicester LE87 4AB
Tel: 01858 438854

ALL ABOUT CATS
Practical Publications Ltd
Suite C
21 Heathmans Road
London SW6 4TJ
Tel: 020 738 43261

UKPETS MAGAZINE ONLINE
www.ukpets.co.uk/ framemag.htm

Glossary and further reading

ANTHROPOMORPHIC

Applies to an animal with human characteristics.

BREED

The subdivision of the domestic species – individuals of the same breed have similar physiological and physical traits and behaviour.

CARNIVORE

Any mammal of the order Carnivora, with jaws and teeth adapted for stabbing, tearing and eating flesh.

CROSS-BREEDING

Mating between different breeds belonging to the same species.

ECOSYSTEM

The balance of plants and animals in a natural environment. Living things develop according to the conditions of the ecosystem around them.

FAMILY

The division of an order of animals or plants. Cats belong to the order of carnivores and to the family of Felidae.

FELIS

The scientific name for the cat genus. Felis catus is the scientific name for the domestic cat.

FERAL

An adjective describing a wild cat, or a domestic cat that has lapsed into a wild state.

GENETICS

The science of heredity and study of variations in inherited characteristics.

HYBRID

An individual produced through cross-breeding or mating between different species.

LINEAGE

The ancestral history of an individual.

MUTATION

The natural or induced change of a transmissible hereditary trait. In the Manx cat, the absence of a tail is a natural mutation.

MICROCHIPPING

A means of pet identification that allows lost pets to be reunited with their owners. A vet inserts a microchip under the skin on the scruff of the cats's neck. The chip emits a unique code, which is held in a central database.

NATURAL SELECTION

The theory of the survival and propagation of organisms best suited to their environment.

OESTRUS

The recurring period of sexual receptivity in female mammals. Cats in oestrus are also referred to as being in season or on heat.

PALPATION

A term used to describe a type of medical examination that involves gentle touching and feeling of the area under investigation.

PEDIGREE

The genealogy of a pure-bred cat or the document stating its origins.

PHEROMONES

The specific scents secreted by female cats from certain glands. A male can tell when a female has passed by, thanks to the phero-mones she leaves by rubbing against things. A female on heat releases sexual pheromones.

SELECTION
*The methods used
to improve a breed by
conserving specific traits
from one generation to
the next.*

SOCIALISATION
*The act of familiarising
an animal with people.*

SPECIES
*A group of individuals
that share the same
characteristics.*

STOP
*The convex area between
a cat's forehead and its
snout. The Persian has a
very marked stop, unlike
the European, which
has only a slight one, and
the Siamese which lacks
it completely.*

TERRITORY
*The domain or
geographical area where
an animal lives.*

Further reading

D. G. Carlson, J. M. Giffin, L. Carlson, *Cat Owner's Home Veterinary Handbook.*
Howell Books Inc, 1995.

Andrew Edney, *101 Essential Tips: Cat Care.*
Dorling Kindersley, 1995.

101 Favourite Cat Poems.
Contemporary Books Inc, 1999.

Sally Franklin, *50 Ways To Train Your Cat.*
Howell Books, 1993.

A. T. B. Edney, Andrew Edney, *Cat: Wild Cats And Pampered Pets.*
Watson-Guptil, 1999.

Katherine M. Rogers, *The Cat And The Human Imagination: Feline Images
From Bast To Garfield.*
University of Michigan Press, 1997.

Roni Jay, *The Kingdom Of The Cat.*
Apple Press, 2000.

Anne Marks, *The Cat In History, Legend And Art.*
Beech Publishing House, 1996.

Carole Wilbourn, *The Total Cat.*
HarperCollins, 2001.

Kathryn Petras, Ross Petras, *Cats: 47 Favourite Breeds, Appearance, History,
Personality and Lore.*
Workman Publishing, 1998.

B. M. Nash, A. Zullo, M. MacFarlane, *Amazing But True Cat Tales.*
Andrews McMeel, 1993.

Contents

Fact ⟫ 2–12
Fun facts and quick quotes

Discover ⟫ 13–44

Look ⟫ 45–66
Cats out and about in Greece …

In practice ⟫ 67–94

Find out ⟫ 95–125

Photo credits

Pg. 14, Sipa Press (ERL) – **Pg. 16–17,** J. L. Charmet – **Pg. 19,** Explorer (Lenars) – **Pg. 20,** SELVA – **Pg. 24,** J. L. Charmet – **Pg. 27,** AKG Paris – **Pg. 28,** MNHN Central Library – **Pg. 31,** Sipa Press (Goldner) – **Pg. 32,** MNHN Central Library – **Pg. 35,** RMN (Chuzeville) – **Pg. 36,** Dagli Orti – **Pg. 39,** Bios (Martin Harvey) – **Pg. 40,** Bios (Hubert Klein) – **Pg. 43,** Bios (J. J. Alcalay) – **Pg. 46–65,** Rapho (Hans Silvester) – **Pg. 66,** Bios (Hubert Klein) – **Pg. 69–94,** Anne Gallet – **Pg. 97,** SELVA – **Pg. 98,** Hachette photocollection – **Pg. 101,** Anne Gallet – **Pg. 102,** KIPA – **Pg. 104–105,** AKG Paris (Maeght Foundation) – **Pg. 107–127,** Anne Gallet.